Remember Me

Re /
mem
/ ber
Me /

Essays /
Lee Zacharias

Unicorn Press / 2024

Copyright © 2024 by Lee Zacharias
All rights reserved

First printing

PAPER   978-0-87775-181-6
CLOTH   978-0-87775-182-3

COVER. Leland River, Michigan; photograph by Lee Zacharias.

∞
This book is printed on Mohawk Via, which is acid-free and meets ANSI standards for archival permanence.

Printed in the United States of America

UNICORN PRESS
Post Office Box 5523
Greensboro, NC 27435

unicorn-press.org

In memory of
James Lester Clark

1945–2017

Remember Me

The Village Idiot	3
Crossing the River	15
Inside the Palace	35
The Bride Beneath My Bed	53

Remember Me

The Village Idiot

HIS NAME WAS WAYNE, and he was seventeen or eighteen the year I was ten, the year my family moved to his neighborhood. He lived up the street, and with the number of houses and years that lay between us, I might never have known him except to recognize him in passing had he been occupied with the usual pursuits of a teenaged boy: cars, girls, job. Wayne was retarded. And yes, that was the term we used back then. His own family used it. We had no idea it might be insensitive or offensive. Word was that he had not been born that way, like the cerebral palsy victim in the neighborhood we had just left, who was nearly as old as I but wore diapers and still slept in a crib; who was fed in a high chair and had to be carried, though she was all limbs and sharp bones; who lolled her head and couldn't speak except to moan and gave me the creeps so bad I had no sympathy for her or her family at all. I had no concept of what it was like not to be normal, a word that can scarcely be used today without quotes, though in 1955 the very letters seemed as solid as pillars. Soon enough, with an awkward adolescence closing in on me, I would come to spend most of my waking hours wishing that *I* was normal, which is to say like everyone else, but the grotesquerie and self-pity of junior high were then still in an unfathomable future—nor when it came did those miseries teach me any more about compassion than they do anyone else of that age.

My mother's explanation was an automobile accident that had caused Wayne's mind to stop growing when he was six, and as if to spite her for the dumbed-down, sweetened literality of her answer to a question I hadn't asked, I imagined his brain to be something like a car stalled out in the intersection while the rest of the world sped past. Other times I pictured the petrified roots at the bottom of our vegetable bin, shriveled beet, shrunken carrot, hard, runkled little gray-green pea rattling around inside his big skull. My brother was six, at which age I was reading circles around my classmates in the first blue Dick-and-Jane primer. No way was Wayne a mental six-year-old, not even three, not any stage we'd passed through, not really. But my mother and I lived in a measured world: budget, report cards, the weekly ten pennies of my allowance, which were kept in a custard cup in a kitchen cabinet. Every time I misbehaved another one was taken away, and when no one was looking, I used to crawl up on the kitchen counter to see how bad I had been. Perhaps my mother thought that the only way I could understand *anything* was to count backwards. It wasn't his fault, we knew, but Wayne didn't have ten pennies.

That there had been an accident I did not doubt. His family had no car, and his father was the only man in the neighborhood to take the bus to work. Rumor held that Mr. Blandford had been driving, that there had been another son killed besides the one who was damaged, that their father refused all his co-workers' offers of carpools and rides because he could not bear ever to enter an automobile again. Every day he walked past our house to and from his bus stop on 173rd Street. On his days off he took the bus to the store and came back bearing two big brown paper bags full of groceries. Every day we watched as he passed, a tired-looking middle-aged man with colorless hair and slumped shoulders.

The houses we lived in were strung down one side of a street that ran for three blocks with no egress. Across the street and up and down the street behind that, the houses belonged to a different tract. On our side they were all cookie-cutter asbestos-shingled three-bedroom, one-bath ranches, with an occasional cedar-shingled maverick slipped onto a lot the developer had apparently failed to acquire. Wayne and I both lived in such maverick houses, but oddball and cookie-cutter alike, we all stared out our picture windows at the picture windows of the two-bedroom brick houses lined up along the other side, like ours minor variations on a theme, two red, then a yellow. Sitting one step higher off the ground and boasting steep gabled roofs for future expansion, they seemed to look down on us. Until she died my mother claimed the two sides of the street had different personalities: ours had always gotten along, but the other, she said, fought "like cats and dogs."

At each end the street was cut off from the rest of the world by routes that passed us by: at the far end a railroad track, at ours a thoroughfare. Behind us, across the dirt alley, were fences. Beyond them the houses that sat with their backs to us were from another era, tall, musty-looking bungalows with English basements and closed-in front porches up steep flights of flaking wooden steps. For forty years they had marked the eastern residential boundary of Hammond, Indiana, turning their backs on the fouled prairie and smokestacks of Gary beyond. Our houses were too new to have grown fences. We had no landscaping, we had no history; we were all of us original owners. Our fathers worked in the steel mills and oil refineries; our mothers stayed home. We were *Leave It to Beaver* without Ward's white-collar wisdom or June's pearls, baby boomers, children born since the War. At ten I was in the front guard; for a while my six-year-old brother brought up the rear, as if we were, like the railroad track and 173rd Street, two poles between which all known forms of the species were clustered.

On our side the backyards stretched the length of those three blocks like a single, unimproved playfield that we roamed with the unimpeachable entitlement of children. If one of us grew peevish and said, "Get out of my yard," the rest of us looked at him blankly. Whatever did he mean, his yard? *We* owned the neighborhood, which meant we also owned Wayne, not because we claimed him but because he claimed us. He was *there*. When we drew a circle in the dirt to shoot marbles, he hunkered in the dust alongside us. If we joined hands for Red Rover, he would slip his rough, meaty palm into ours. He played tag with us, he played hopscotch, he played Mother May I, but he didn't jump rope and he didn't play dolls. I used to spread my plastic dollhouse furniture across the back stoop and invite him to join me just to see him back down the walk, a look of profound discomfiture on his face as he said in his flat, booming voice, "Nah, that stuff's for girls." He preferred running games, to which he brought a sloppy strength that was at once a lope and a gallop, and his face lit with joy each time Red Rover called him over and he burst through our flimsy human chains. Competition made him giddy, though he could never remember who was on which side or which side was winning. He was awful at everything, of course. He forgot the rules, he was clumsy, he was too big, he was too old, he didn't *fit* us. "Oh Wayne," we would scold, "Oh Wayne," the neighborhood's collective sigh. "Cut it out, Wayne, stop, Wayne, don't, you're going to break it." If he was wounded by the shortness of our tempers he didn't show it. In the forty-some years he spent on our street I never saw him in a bad mood.

We didn't know his brother or sister. The brother was a handsome boy of fourteen or fifteen who spent his time riding around with friends in cars, already hopelessly indifferent to children and their games. As I recall, his sister's name was Susie. She was much younger, somewhere near my brother's age, though she never joined us at play. She snubbed us, as if, like her handsome brother, she considered us childish and vulgar. She was a pretty girl, small and blonde, *spoiled* we heard our parents whisper, *a prima donna, what else would you expect?* and when Wayne followed her down the street, we could hear her scream, "Leave me alone! Go home! Get away from me, dummy!" I imagine now how she must have hated her childhood, the nightly dinners in the dull, flattened light of a kitchen made stuffy by the grease that hung in the air, staring at the empty place for the brother who was, at fourteen or fifteen, already never there, stranded at the Formica table that would have had to be squeezed up against the wall, listening to the scrape of their forks and insufferable sound of their chewing, the parents who would never drive her anywhere and the other brother, the dummy, the retard, the one who would never be gone.

Who could blame her? Though we did. Not for her cruelty to Wayne, but for her unforgivable dismissal of us.

IT SEEMS TO ME now that we knew everything about one another and yet very little, for so much of what appeared to be our real life, children's and adults' alike, took place in daylight, in the public space of the street. We rarely entered one another's houses. By day we children belonged to the frontier of our childhood, the long stretch of backyards and weedy vacant lot at 173rd Street that we called our prairie. Summoned home for supper, we retreated to the cramped civilization of our families. Nights, Beech Avenue was lit by the ashy flicker of our small black-and-white TVs. Our living rooms rang with the tinny sound of canned laughter. In our families' apprehension of the mute darkness that reclaimed the world outside, our secret lives took place.

The peeping Tom was a shadow, an apparition, a whisper. A presence only my mother could feel, he was the dark hiss inside her voice and an angry black light in her eye, a rustle at the edge of night, a clotted breath and sudden denseness in the air. He was more than a threat; he was an accusation, both the evil that lurked outside and the uncharted maleficence waiting inside me, for I was ten, eleven, and twelve, after all. On the cusp of adolescence I must have seemed to my mother both imperiled and precipitous. I liked to write, and beneath the socks in my underwear drawer I hid a notebook that contained my novel-in-progress, which my mother removed each day to read, just as she read the locked diary I kept in my nightstand, searching for clues not to who I was but to whom I must be prevented from becoming.

She believed that Wayne was the peeping Tom, and his name in her mouth turned the shape of both ugly. He was a nasty secret, hers and mine, like her menstrual blood, my failings, my father's perpetual disappointment in my brother, and the malignant will between my parents. The police were never called. My mother had no evidence. Nor did she voice her fears to the neighbors. What would have been the point? For the cookie-cut houses that lined our side of the street had impenetrable bedroom windows, narrow rectangles of glass set high as transoms in the walls. On the entire length of our side of Beech Avenue, I possessed the single vulnerable window, cut deep into my bedroom wall.

Still she *knew*, or thought she did, though what she knew I received in a tangle of fragments and festering implications. To her it was matter of logic. Wayne might have the mind of a child, but he had a man's body, I heard her whisper to my father. He had *urges*, she warned me, her voice twisting on the dark mystery coiled inside the word. It was not that she had anything against him, she said in the same slightly sanctimonious tone she reserved for all the lectures on difference and tolerance that her behavior contradicted, a tone that claimed credit for being fair at heart even if reality demanded a different course of action, the same tone I would hear several years later when I made plans to get together with a Black college friend from Gary one Christmas vacation and my mother refused to allow her to visit our house. My mother had nothing against my friend Gigi either.

I had no sense of what *urges* Wayne might have, only that they were unspeakably depraved, and that we were responsible, he and I both, for the rancor in her voice and the mute, angry red flush beneath her skin. He had no business playing with girls, she huffed, and though she could not forbid me to play with Wayne— for to do so would have been to forbid me to play with anyone at all—I was not allowed to play with him alone. I don't know what she thought should be done. Once the live-in grandmother of the cerebral palsy victim in our previous neighborhood, who blamed her daughter-in-law for the defective child, had snapped that the girl was a freak who belonged in an institution with other freaks, a rebuke my mother reported with considerable dander, for she and the girl's mother were friends. But the poor girl in her crib and diapers posed no threat to us. My mother could hardly knock on the Blandfords' door to demand that they send Wayne away. Nor could she rally her neighbors, for what could she say? That once, glancing into the backyard at dusk, she might have seen a moving shadow. Or perhaps what she saw was just the shape of her own fear.

I was not afraid of Wayne. If I was uneasy with him it was because I was uneasy with my own confusion and guilt, for I think I knew all along that he was no peeping Tom. Not the Wayne we knew, so enthusiastic and ungainly he would have been incapable of stealth, an oaf, a lummox with disjointed limbs and overgrown feet. Though the rest of his family were small people, short, slender, fair of hair, and delicate in feature, as if to compensate for his stunted brain, Wayne had grown tall and lanky and seemed crudely made. He walked on the balls of his feet in a loose, bobbing stride that seemed to pitch him forward, and he had the loud, inflectionless voice of the hearing impaired, a man's voice, growly and deep, a bass had he known how to carry a tune, which we all learned he could not when later he joined the Woodmar Church of God at the corner, where the sound of Wayne hollering out the hymns spilled through the yellow-lit windows on warm summer nights. He was ridiculous, this oversized man-child waving a washed-out mayonnaise jar with holes punched in the lid as he chased down lightning bugs with a gaggle of six-year-olds. He had a heavy beard, and his face was perpetually dark with five o'clock shadow, but his brown hair was unruly as a boy's, full of cowlicks, unevenly chopped. His clothes never fit, though it was less a matter of size than the unfashionable cut of those J.C. Penney twills and the way he wore them, plaid shirttails hanging out, pants cinched high at the waist, bagging at the knees, flapping at his ankles. Halloweens he ran trick-or-treating from house to house with us, the real bones of his ankles and wrists protruding like a pun from the white skeleton printed on the flimsy black acetate of his dime-store coverall. Large and dark, his eyes had a raw, slick, wet glister, locked in an unblinking stare as steady as a cheap camera's fixed focus. He didn't have the sense to be self-conscious. And so he scratched where he itched, picked his nose, licked his lips, and never ever looked away.

When we were at school, he sought out the company of our mothers, making the rounds up and down the block, crossing from one side of the street to the other, stopping in for candy, cookies, milk, or a glass of pop. If a family sat out on their stoop to catch the breeze on a summer evening, Wayne would seat himself on the steps alongside them. If one of our fathers raised a car hood to tinker, Wayne would be there for a look. If someone went to Wolf Lake or Willow Slough and came home with a pile of perch or blue gills to clean, Wayne would arrive to pitch in, though all he was allowed to do was watch, reporting to the next-door neighbors how many and what kind, waiting until the last head had been wrapped in newspaper and taken out to the trash, smacking his lips and rubbing his stomach in anticipation, though he was never invited to the family fish fry, and when his mother called, he obediently trotted home to supper. He was a good boy, she said; he never gave her any trouble. The one person on the street who could enter nearly every house, he bore bulletins from one end to the other and back again, crossing to and from the brick houses on the other side with the neighborhood news, who was going on vacation or out to dinner, who had an anniversary, who was expecting, later who had cancer or was getting a divorce. We knew the affairs of families we'd never met, families who lived so far down the street we did not recognize them when they passed.

He did go away for a while, to a special school that he rode the bus to each day. His parents must have despaired of his learning skills that would allow him to hold a job and become independent, but the school gave him something to do, just as church did a few years later. They couldn't count on us to keep him entertained, for even as children each weekday from September through June we left him, crossing the vacant lot beside the church and walking the two blocks to Wilson School. Later, when our prairie fell to a variety store, then a laundromat and a bakery, we shopped at Joe Kay's, lingering in the aisles until Joe Kay signaled it was time to leave by asking if we were going to buy anything. We rode our bikes around the corner, down Chestnut, and into the world beyond. Eventually we went off to jobs or, a very few of us, to college. We moved to Iowa and California, to Texas and North Carolina. The steel belt turned into the rust belt, and the value of our parents' houses dropped. Those who wanted to leave, who dreamed of retiring to Florida or buying a condo, couldn't afford to. There weren't that many children to replace us.

It seems ironic that my mother should have fretted over Wayne for fear of my impending adolescence, for had I needed to be protected, adolescence would have served. If he would never outgrow us, we were destined to outgrow him. Already my days in the gang of neighborhood children were numbered. One snowless winter day we all sat behind the Flemings' garage and built an elaborate landscape of mountains, tunnels, and roads in the cold, hard-packed sand of the alley, filling it with a traffic jam of miniature cars and trucks. Nothing but dirt and dye-stamped metal for our tools, yet we created a world so full of childhood magic it transported us from the dingy reality of the neighborhood around us, the small, drab houses, the garbage cans and oil drums that lined the alley, the sky that was always the color of smoke from the mills, the reddened eyes and grimy faces of the fathers who stoked their fires, and the worn voices of our mothers calling us home. Beside me Wayne squatted in the dirt, the car in his hand a chipped turquoise or orange, not a Matchbox classic but the kind so cheap a single color covers even the windshield and bumpers. "Vroom, vroom," he growled, a deep rumble inside his throat, as he drove that blind, engineless car as far as it would take him. The next day, it seemed, I bought a teen magazine at Joe Kay's, or perhaps I took the bus downtown and in the basement bins of Goldblatt's selected my first forty-five, Ricky Nelson singing "Poor Little Fool" or Elvis begging me to love him tender. At home I placed it on the secondhand hi-fi in our basement and practiced dancing, and while Wayne and the other children played on outside, I waltzed off into adolescence and the adult life beyond.

So it came to nothing, the peeping Tom, my mother's fears. One by one we grew up. Wayne found the church, and when we came home for visits, we saw him playing with the new children, few as they were, though more and more he spent his time with our parents, far more faithful to them than we could ever be, unchanging as he was year after year, a constant in a neighborhood of remarkable constancy. More than sixty years have passed since my family moved to Beech Avenue, but until my mother's next-door neighbor to the south died in 1990 there was an unbroken chain of eight houses still occupied by original owners. Inevitably the chain grew shorter until my mother was the only one left. Wayne's parents have been gone for years. Though they must have dreaded the day when they would have to leave him, they couldn't prevent it. First his father died; then his mother succumbed to Alzheimer's and had to be removed to a nursing home, no longer able to care for her son, no longer certain who he was. An aunt called his brother and sister, but neither was willing to take him in.

I was visiting that summer while the aunt stayed in the house with him to wait for a place to open in a group home, and I felt a rise of the old animosity we had borne his sister. He was sixty years old; for nearly half a century Beech Avenue had been his whole world. "How can he be expected to leave it and adjust to another?" I fumed to my mother, who agreed. She might have forgotten she once wished him gone. Did she remember how she suspected him? I don't know. It is not something I would have asked.

That evening when Wayne passed on his neighborhood rounds, I went down the front walk to meet him. I told him I was sorry about his mother. "Yah," he said in his flat, open voice. Then he pointed to the sky and grinned. "They're up there, waitin' for me." And it occurred to me that perhaps what we had always taken for a fool's undiscriminating cheer was genuine optimism, less ignorance than grace. Save a small, grizzled patch of gray at his temples, he looked much the same as he had when I was ten, but I had changed so much that I could barely remember the girl I'd been, and so I asked, "Do you know me?" "Yah," he said and jerked his hand toward my mother's house. "You're Dorothy's daughter."

A dozen years had passed since I'd last heard that phrase. I had been visiting my mother then too; it was a soft August night, and after supper I had taken a walk. Across the street Wayne was sitting with Irene Ihnat's family in the circle of lawn chairs in her front yard. I knew Irene because she had worked for my mother in the cafeteria of Wilson School, a plump, pretty, pink-cheeked woman with a sweet smile, sparkling blue eyes, and silver hair, though she'd been stricken with brain cancer since I had last eaten lunch with my mother's staff, and for the three or four years she lingered after she was lobotomized, my mother's letters obsessed on the pathos of her condition, each one noting what a blessing it would be if she just died. In those years after her surgery, Irene's sister liked to bring her out to the yard on clement evenings. Wayne was chatting with Irene's husband when her sister called me over. "It's Dorothy's daughter. Say hello," she said sternly to Irene. At length the thin, bald woman slumped in a wheelchair raised her head and stared balefully at me. I was terrified. Though her skin was an ashy yellow and her body no more than a pile of sticks, her eyes held the fierce, sucking black force of the grave. "Say hello," Irene's sister ordered again, but the power of death's rage was spent, and the stranger's head dropped back to her chest. A year or two later she died, my mother found a new obsession, and more than a decade had passed, but suddenly I was Dorothy's daughter again, sitting in that circle of folding chairs on Irene's lawn at the same time I stood on the walk in front of my mother's house with Wayne.

"It's good to see you," I told him. And in the next years, as more of the original owners died off and my mother began the journey to her own decline, I have wondered did he count the time between those visits the way I did, not by accomplishments, of course, not by the arc of a career or growth of one's child, but in the way we all come to count the years in the end, by our losses. "Yah," he said. I told him goodbye, wished him well in his new home, came inside, and cried.

A few months later, when I asked my mother if she had heard how Wayne was doing, she told me he was happy. His aunt had brought him back for a visit, and he had gone from neighbor to neighbor, reporting to everyone how much he liked his new home. "Would you believe it's the neighborhood that's had trouble adjusting?" she said, her voice climbing. "People miss him, they really do. Would you believe we actually grieved?"

When I remember the surprise in her voice, I think of the story my friend and colleague Jim Clark told me about the retarded boy in the neighborhood where he grew up in Miami, in that same era, before we learned not to speak of the retarded but of people with special needs. There is always a special-needs child or childlike adult, it seems. In European folklore nearly every village has its "idiot." According to a beloved Yiddish tale, when God created the world He sent an angel with a bag of fools to distribute throughout his masterpiece, but the angel tripped, the bag broke, and they all fell to the ground in what is now Poland, where they founded the village of Chelm. Paul was theirs, down in South Florida, a kind of holy fool as Jim described him, for by instinct the other children knew he belonged to them, that he was theirs to protect. He may have had a stroke; he was partially crippled on one side, and his palsied hand slapped against his bare thigh with a terrible pocking sound when he walked. Jim grew up detesting the sound, though it was what he missed most when he returned years later for his mother's funeral and learned that Paul had died. The neighborhood seemed so unbearably silent, he said.

Perhaps six years after Wayne had moved I asked my mother if he still came back to visit. "Wayne?" she said as if his memory had grown so distant she was trying to place him. "Oh no. Never. He was very happy though." And then she rushed on to tell me the latest about the greedy children of a neighborhood friend in failing health who had become her current cause. Each time I phoned, I was reminded that the people who settled Beech Avenue were disappearing, that among those who were left and those who replaced them, there was no one to carry the news back and forth, no one to make them feel that the small daily events of their lives had the significance of news, no one to connect them. There were so many new neighbors my mother no longer knew their names. We were mistaken to think Wayne stalled in time, as if he would not travel with us. All these years he has been by our sides, though we were so blinded by our futures, so arrogant with health and certain of our luck, we did not know it was the idiot who made us a village.

Crossing the River

I

THERE WAS NO ONE who could say *hell* like my father-in-law. It was the relish he gave the word, the emphasis, the zest. At once cheery and dismissive, the syllable exploded in his mouth, a brief but vigorous announcement that there would be no bullshit in the sentence that followed. Should we deal him in for the next hand? "Hell yes." Would he want to make a little wager on the football scores? "Hell, he could have had third," he would say, watching a baseball game in our den; "Hell, we've got an ocean right here," when North Carolina objected to piping water from Lake Gaston to Virginia Beach. One of his favorite stories was about the funeral for a former landlord who had lived upstairs on 28th Street in Norfolk when my husband, Michael, was small. Michael remembers the landlord as an impeccably dressed Shriner who smoked Between the Acts cigarillos that came in a transfixing red-lettered palm-sized gold tin, though apparently Harry was something of a scoundrel. Tears of delight would spring to my father-in-law's eyes as he mimicked the rolling *r*'s and mincing accent of the eulogist, who rose to say, "One thing you could say about Haarrry, Haarrry had *principles*." Here my father-in-law always broke into a sputtered laugh. "Hell, Harry didn't have any principles. The only thing you could say about Harry was that Harry was a bum."

He was not a profane man. *Hell* and *damn* were the only four-letter words I ever heard him use, and on his tongue they were less obscenities than expressions of his gregarious, cut-to-the-chase nature. He was a lay reader for the Episcopal Church who lived in the world of the practical and never spoke of the spirit, a gentleman with courtly manners but little use for squeamishness or pretension, who once gave me an aerosol can labeled "bullshit repellant" to keep on the desk of my university office. The excesses of politicians and sports figures especially amused him, and he had no reverence for the social pieties that brighten up death. His own father died young. An Italian immigrant born in Uruguay, he perished in the flu epidemic of 1918, leaving his pretty Italian widow with four young sons. My father-in-law was five, and one of his earliest memories was of his father laid out on the kitchen table while the mourners got drunk and chased their mother around the corpse until she shooed them out with a broom and they fell in a merry heap in the snow at the bottom of the steps. "Hell, they were so drunk they couldn't walk home," he would say, laughing along with them.

    In his eighties my father-in-law began to turn the word *hell* on himself, a kind of breezy reality check whenever he found himself indulging in plans. Though he had grown up in Pennsylvania and Michigan, he hated cold weather, and for the last fourteen years of his life he wintered in the Florida Keys, in an apartment beneath his younger son's house, though new FEMA regulations that followed Hurricane Andrew threatened to eliminate his winter abode. Sometimes he spoke of renovations that would raise the concrete floor; occasionally he talked of renting a room at the marina where my brother-in-law worked as a fishing guide. How strict the proposed codes would be was still a matter of debate, but whenever he caught himself entertaining his options overlong, he would interrupt himself with a brisk, "What the hell, I'll be crossing the river soon." When the need for diuretics forced him to give up his long strolls on the beach, when he stopped driving, when he told us he could no longer visit North Carolina—the stairs of our old house were too much—whenever age deprived him of another of his pleasures, it was always, "Hell, I'll be crossing the river soon." He made the passage sound no more complicated, no more to be feared, than a trip to the grocery store. Years before, he had prepaid his funeral arrangements, which included a private viewing for the family, "So you can make sure that it's me." Michael had instructions to tuck a notebook and pencil in his pocket, in case my father-in-law saw anything he wanted to write down on the other side. He'd taken care of everything. All he had to do was die.

If my mother-in-law, a gracious and gentle woman who suffered from depression as well as emphysema, had any complaint about a husband who took such excellent care of her that he never left her for more than a half-hour walk, it would have been that his cheer was relentless. Her relationship with her mother had been difficult, and in her later years she began to obsess on old slights, assigning my father-in-law the task of expressing her grievances to her siblings back in Michigan, which he did with his own spin. "Hell, Seymour, I'm seventy-two years old," he said after relaying her sentiments to her brother. "What do I care about the past? All I want is my bowl of ice cream." Bowl was an understatement, for he never did anything halfway, and when my mother-in-law's health forced her to give up drinking, he replaced his daily martinis with ice cream concoctions so immense he christened them "aircraft carriers." "Savor every bite," he advised his grandsons, pronouncing the word with a short *a*, as if the shortened syllable might make the advice apply not just to ice cream or dinner but to life. "That's nice!" was another of his pet sayings until his wife grew so weary of the words she forbade him ever to use them again. He replaced them with "You're beautiful," to which, I imagine, she found it hard to object.

It was her death that freed him to winter in the Keys. The week before she died, fresh out of the hospital, she had called us, vowing to stay in closer touch. "Once those boys were my whole life, and now I hardly ever talk to them," she said, a statement so inaccurate that it struck me even then as an omen. The next weekend she was back in the hospital. The last time my father-in-law saw her conscious was Sunday night, and when my husband asked what her last words had been, he told us she'd asked if the Redskins won. Though he was a Redskins—now Commanders—fan himself, Michael seemed disappointed. "You mean the last thing you told her was the football score?" No doubt he had hoped for something a little more momentous, more suiting the solemnity of a long goodbye, but my father-in-law was oblivious, characteristically matter-of-fact. After all, they'd had a good marriage—"A nice house, nice cars, nice kids—you can't ask for more than that," he said later, summing up their life together— and anything that needed to be said between them would have been said long before. Only once did I see his composure crack. Sitting at the kitchen table, speaking about her two or three days after her death, he burst into tears. A minute later he apologized for "losing himself" and went on with his factual account of her last day. There was no eulogy at her graveside service, an omission that greatly troubled my husband. When it was over, my father-in-law set his jaunty, checkered wool fedora atop her coffin with a friendly rap of his knuckles, as if to say *Hi, how are you doing in there?* before stepping out to greet the mourners. "I told her I was going to do that," he confided to me.

We had always spent Thanksgiving in Virginia Beach, but now the visit began with a trip to a florist for the single red rose Michael would take to the cemetery. My father-in-law didn't see the point. "She's got flowers," he said, referring to the silk bouquet he kept in the small urn on the grave, a double berth with a bronze plaque on a flat pink granite stone needing only the date of his death to be filled in. "Together forever" it promises. Every so often he brought the flowers home to wash, and he kept a sharp knife and a dandelion fork in a wrinkled brown paper bag labeled "cemetery implements" in black Magic Marker, the same bag that now resides in the trunk of my husband's car. Sometimes they cleaned the grave together, though Michael complained it was hard to maintain a mood of mourning with his father along. Once, when I went with them, my father-in-law leapt on the stone, bouncing up and down in his white Reeboks, demanding gleefully, "Take a picture of me standing on my grave."

He could be impetuous. Within days of his wife's death he sold the family house and bought into a high-rise senior facility on Chesapeake Bay called Westminster, where he spent the last fourteen years of his life in a one-room eighth-floor apartment overlooking the Lynnhaven Fishing Pier, a lock-and-go place that offered a full social life and assisted living or health care should the need ever arise. The day after her funeral he took us to visit, introducing himself to the residents with the same exuberance a presidential candidate brings to the stump. We had always viewed the place with distaste, for we'd watched the imposing brick edifice rise over the ruins of seedy mom-and-pop motels along a strip of beach we frequented with my stepson when he was young, but in the end it would prove a practical decision. He enjoyed the place immensely. He played Scrabble with a group of ladies after making it clear that he had had a long and satisfying marriage and wouldn't be looking for romantic attachments, though the same ladies were forbidden to join him and his cronies at the dinner table, where, he assured them, they wouldn't appreciate the randy jokes and ribald comments of the all-male camaraderie. He wrote and illustrated humorous anecdotes for Westminster's newsletter, helped call the bingo games and staffed the flotsam-and-jetsam sales, fundraisers whose merchandise consisted of unclaimed possessions from the apartments of the deceased. Most of all he relished the lively fellowship of the poolroom, also off-limits to women, where he honed his skills to win the championship, skills he undoubtedly called "surgical maneuvers" after the moves he once made on the shuffleboard court in his driveway before a hernia put an end to his shuffleboard career. You couldn't beat him, not at shuffleboard, not at pool, not at cards. In the '30s, when he played second base for the Marine All-Stars, his teammates called him the Mighty Mite; in the oversized photograph of him that hangs on our dining room wall, he stands with hands on the hips of his Saginaw High School football pants, so handsome, so sturdy and resolute you would never guess he was only five feet seven. An ardent Democrat who might have gone into local politics had his wife had the stamina for it, he thrived on competition. "Shall we tickle the pasteboards, boys and girls?" he would ask each evening we visited, as if we didn't already know that we were going to spend the next hour or two playing penny-ante poker. His favorite game was low hole card, which he called over and over; if one of us slapped down three aces, my father-in-law would have a "little straight"; if someone had a straight he would have a flush. "Thank you, boys," he would say, sweeping the pot toward him with a sly smile as he sat in what he called his Sparky jacket, a regulation Detroit Tigers warm-up that I gave my husband one Christmas and he in turn gave to his father, for my father-in-law had loved the Tigers even longer than Michael and in his last years he was always cold. Sitting in his Sparky jacket, raking in his pennies, reveling in our half-complimentary remarks about his luck, he wore that smile like a secret, the secret of his luck. He had a talent for it that was, I think, the same talent for his cheer. Everyone loved him, and he knew it.

When congestive heart failure made his feet swell, he cut slits in the tops of his Reeboks, a solution the other residents of Westminster thought so clever they asked if he wouldn't customize their shoes too. He added an extender to his shoehorn so he wouldn't have to bend over and wrapped his toenail clippers with adhesive tape for a comfortable grip. He collected rubber bands for every imaginable use, and when he died, among the meager possessions in his apartment, I found a giant pill bottle full of rubber bands and in his bathroom a family-sized bottle of Listerine. For as long as Michael could remember his father had washed his hair with Listerine, since shampoo wouldn't do to rinse his mouth, and there was no sense in buying two products when one would do. In his drawer was a ledger listing every expense of his adult life. Yet when he sold the family house, in his eagerness to move to Westminster, he gave away my mother-in-law's beautiful furniture and nearly abandoned her crystal, which I rescued from a cupboard over the refrigerator and packed in a cardboard box. Though he had walked me through the rooms the day after her funeral, speaking of how the possessions should be divvied up, by the following week, when we returned to help, the house had already been sold. The neighbor who bought it, "just drooled when she saw the furniture," he reported, "so I said hell, as far as I'm concerned, the furniture goes with the house." "Hell, leave it for the Newhalls," he said when I climbed on a chair to find the crystal, but the stack of empty margarine tubs beneath the counter was another matter. "Can you use these?" he wanted to know. *Use* was an operating word for him, and though I wish I had my mother-in-law's Chippendale dining room suite, her blue-and-white bun-footed sofa and gorgeous crewel chairs, the truth is he would not live on in those things. What he inhabits are the humble implements he used—the electric knife with which my husband now carves the roast, an appliance more than half a century old, still stored in its original box; the aluminum colander I use to drain pasta, the kind I once bought at Woolworth's for a dollar and later discarded, replacing it with an expensive stainless steel model that never did drain right; his chopping board; his tongs.

For years after my mother-in-law's death he carried her hot pink Samsonite suitcase and matching train case; it would never have occurred to him to be embarrassed by the color, for it was perfectly usable luggage. He replaced it only when he stopped driving, for on a plane he would have had to check the Pullman. Every December he flew to Miami with everything he needed for four months in the Keys in a green canvas carry-on and the tan briefcase that had held his irrigation supplies ever since his surgery for colon cancer thirty years before. He might expect to cross the river soon, but he'd dipped a toe into that water before, and he was glad to be alive.

2

THERE WERE TWO CAMPS on my father-in-law's name. Everyone called my mother-in-law Madre, which appears on her tombstone beneath her given name and dates. My father-in-law's given name was Alman. His father, Giuseppi Vittorio Gaspardone, had changed the family name to Gaspeny when he left the coal mines of Pennsylvania to work for the railroad. But it was not the altered surname on which his children differed, even though late in life his brother Lawrence began to sign his own name Lorenzo Gaspardone. It was the nickname, not Al as he was called by his friends, but Pap, the one that appears on his grave beneath his given name and dates. He was Pap to my brother-in-law and his wife and the large circle of their friends who used to hang out in the kitchen of the house in Virginia Beach before my brother-in-law moved to the Keys, Pap to the teenaged boy he took in as a foster child after my husband left home and to the boy's brothers, but to us he was Koke, a name my stepson, also Al, named Alman for his grandfather, bestowed upon him when he was a tot. All of my father-in-law's letters and cards to us were signed Koke, all to my brother-in-law and his wife signed Pap, as if he were one father to his first son and another to the other.

There was the younger son who brought all his friends home to socialize with his parents, who lived at home while attending Old Dominion University, who married late and never divorced, the fishing guide whose deeds—the world records and awards—filled the sports pages of the *Virginian Pilot*, which once featured a picture of Vic and my father-in-law holding matching snook under the headline "He took Dad fishing." The story recounted how he had driven Vic to Cape Hatteras every weekend for years after my brother-in-law outgrew the Tidewater lakes and piers; "My father is my best friend," Vic told the reporter. And there was the other son, who also loved his father, but preferred to hang out at a friend's house while he was growing up, who went away to school and came home married, a father himself at twenty-two, whose obligations and affections traveled down the line and not just up, the college professor who had to endure the awkward silences of the cronies at Westminster whenever my father-in-law introduced "my son" and they gushed, "Oh, the fishing guide," and he had to answer, "No, the teacher."

To name something is to stake a claim. When I am with my sister-in-law, and she speaks of Pap, I hesitate. Why not? We are, after all, talking about someone we shared, and I feel as if I am distancing myself when I say Koke, as if I am insisting on a point I don't fully understand, a point I've never quite seen the need for making. I feel like my father-in-law, relaying his wife's resentments: What do I care about a past in which I was not present? And yet, much as I love my sister-in-law, I cannot put the word *Pap* in my mouth, for on my tongue it would taste not just of falsity but betrayal. I cannot give away my husband's father.

3

IT WAS KOKE'S OUTLOOK, of course, that made him seem so invulnerable to age. "Can you believe how well he's doing?" Michael asked after each visit, and he was, though the harbingers were there if you chose to see them. He began to take my arm when we walked. He no longer arrived at our house with a request for a list of chores—the lawnmowers and faucets and latches in need of fixing—instead he donned an apron and polished my silver, and then he no longer did that. He had cataract surgery, but, "Hell, that's nothing." He got a nasty case of shingles. Finally he was diagnosed with congestive heart failure. "I've got so many little things wrong with me I don't do too much anymore," he confided as he unfolded his lawn chair in the carport in the Keys and we rushed off to the Wild Bird Center or Anne's Beach or the canoe trails at Long Key, wherever we would spend the hours before dinner and his nightly triumph at cards.

Michael was out, teaching a night class, and I was in the middle of hosting a cocktail party for a job candidate when Vic called to report that my father-in-law had had a transient ischemic attack, or ministroke. He was put on Coumadin. Though he would not have another TIA for more than eleven years, the call proved prophetic, for in the coming years it would always be Vic who made the calls, we who were never home waiting. And though it was inevitable that Vic would become the keeper of his father's health—my father-in-law spent so much time in the Keys; Vic and Linda vacationed a month or two of every fall in Virginia Beach; Linda is a nurse—by distance, by default, we became the truants.

My father-in-law had a pacemaker installed. He had surgery for his hernia. He had a carotid endarterectomy. Six weeks before the endarterectomy he arrived in North Carolina grumpy with a cold, complaining of a canker sore, so querulous we scarcely knew him. To please him I promised to cook some fried rice—he loved Chinese food—but before I could finish dicing the vegetables he wanted tea, and then while I was heating the wok he demanded a straw. The tea was too hot; his cold sore hurt. "If you can't give me a straw right now, you might as well just throw it down the sink," he said. As I opened a drawer to search, the wok caught fire, flames shot to the ceiling, and I had to snatch it from the stove and drop it in the sink. I brought dinner to the table with my burnt forearm wrapped in a towel. "Where's my straw?" he demanded. "Dad!" Michael shouted. "Can't you see she's hurt?" "I don't care," he insisted. That fall surgeons reamed out his artery, and I never heard him complain about anything again until he was dying.

When he was eighty-six years old, he was struck by a bicycle while walking along the asphalt trail that runs beside the highway on Plantation Key and knocked to the ground. Though no bones were broken, his face was badly lacerated and his body severely bruised; he lost a lot of blood and never did regain his color. He had always loved to walk, but from then on he walked with a cane. He grew a beard to cover the scars from the gravel embedded in his chin and boasted to us that people told him he looked so distinguished with his walking stick and beard they thought he was a college professor. It did not seem to register that my husband and I actually were professors. That Christmas, when Mike mentioned that he planned to visit an old friend in Detroit the next summer, Koke immediately volunteered to go along. He wanted to see his brother Lawrence. They could take in some Tigers games with Michael's friend and drive on to Traverse City, a boys' trip just like old times, the many summers when he and Michael had driven to Arkansas together to see my stepson Al. It was not the trip Michael had in mind, but how could he object?

Later that winter Koke developed a cough he couldn't shake; he didn't feel good; he was anemic. But he wanted to see his last surviving brother, so perhaps he wouldn't let Vic call. Or perhaps Vic did call, mentioning only that Pap had a cold. We were distracted that spring—I had bronchitis, my mother was hospitalized, our son Max survived a bad auto accident. Koke said nothing about his health when he called to finalize their plans. They were to leave the morning after Max's high school graduation. Both my mother and Al were flying in; Michael and Al would drive to Virginia Beach to fetch Koke, though on the appointed morning they were delayed by a flat tire, and when they finally arrived back in Greensboro, Michael had to help his father into the backyard, where my mother and I were sitting by our pond. He had lost weight; his voice was weak, his face gaunt, his skin gray; he had a nasty cough and scarcely seemed aware of where he was. "Mike can't take him to Michigan," my mother whispered to me. "He'll never make it." He didn't make it through the graduation, which Michael missed in order to bring his father home; nor did he make it through the Tigers games when they reached Detroit, but he was determined to see his brother.

And he rallied in Traverse City, where he and Michael took an enormous liking to Lawrence's son-in-law, Larry. But the trip was hard on both of them, and when the car broke down on the way back, my father-in-law broke down too. He was sick, he wanted to go home. It was a Saturday night; the following day would be both Father's Day and his eighty-eighth birthday, though he saw nothing to celebrate on a day when garages would be closed. But when Michael called to warn me that I would probably need to drive to Ohio to get him, I was still entertaining my mother, who had missed her flight two days before, refused to board a later one, and now declined to leave. By the time Michael got his father back to Virginia Beach, they were barely speaking.

A week later he felt better, though he called to tell us that Larry had died of an aneurism. But he wanted to thank Michael for the trip, for everything Michael had done for him. He seemed a little sheepish; perhaps that's why he didn't tell us when he began to feel worse. On September 11, as we watched the World Trade Center collapse again and again, Vic called to report that he was in the hospital with a cough and general weakness. Though his doctor refused to test for tuberculosis, he did agree to a transfusion, and in early October, when Mike drove to Virginia Beach to watch a Redskins game with his father, Koke felt much brighter. I had sprained my knee and was writing the College Teaching Excellence Lecture, which I was to deliver to the university on October 30, so had to settle for sending a card. He liked cards. He would open one and read it slowly out loud, as if savoring the message. "Very nice," he would say, then rip it in half and drop it in the garbage. "You need to get well. There is no one who can say hell like you do," I wrote, imagining how he would laugh. Later, when he was dying and no longer able to speak, when a friend came to his room to pray for him, praying at such length I almost said when he left, "Man, I thought that guy was never going to quit praying," then thought better, I would wonder if he had laughed after all.

Vic and Linda had returned to Florida. And so it was not Vic but the Westminster nurse who called at the end of October to report that my father-in-law was very weak, confused, frightened, and lonely. He was admitted to the hospital with pneumonia, and the next day Vic called from the Keys, first to say that Pap had been given only a few days to live, then a couple of weeks, and finally to report that even though the doctor did not believe my father-in-law had it, he was beginning treatment for TB. When we arrived at the hospital Koke acknowledged us with the silent, beady stare of the near-dead; only when the outdoor columnist from the *Virginian Pilot* who had written so many stories about my brother-in-law appeared in the doorway did he speak. "Hello, Bob," he said. A few minutes later an ambulance took him back to Westminster. When he woke, he wasn't sure where he was; I had to promise him over and over that he was in Westminster's Health Care before he understood he was no longer in the hospital. His face turned rosy. "You're beautiful!" he said. He wanted to get up, and his voice gained strength as I helped him from the bed to a chair. By morning, he had a list of errands for me—he needed a bathrobe, pajamas, and some slipper socks. As soon as he was well enough to leave Health Care he planned to move to Assisted Living; all he wanted was a promise that we wouldn't send him back to the hospital. By the time Vic, Linda, and Max reached Virginia Beach—hoping just to get there in time—he was ready to walk, and when we got him to the doorway he zipped down the hall with my sister-in-law clinging to his belt. The following day we all watched his beloved team as he presided from the bed in his Redskins cap. He was in excellent spirits when Michael and I drove back to Greensboro Monday evening—the Skins had beat the Seahawks, the Yankees had lost the World Series, Vic and Linda were still there, and though we had to teach our classes, we would be back the next weekend. In a few weeks, I promised, we would have Thanksgiving together just like always.

But on Wednesday he had a ministroke, and when we arrived on Saturday morning, he was babbling. "I don't know where he is," my sister-in-law said, wiping her eyes, "but he's happy." Though he was still incoherent when we left on Sunday night, after my classes on Tuesday afternoon, when I drove back alone, I found him lucid and wheelchair-mobile. He'd had lunch in the Health Care dining room for the first time and was still vexed that the staff had made him take off his ball cap and wouldn't let him have wine.

Vic and Linda had to return to Florida to keep their health insurance. And so in the end it was the older son who became his father's keeper. For the next month Michael and I would spend every weekend in Virginia Beach; because I had no Wednesday classes, I would make the 530-mile round trip midweek alone. Sometimes I arrived to find him strong and clear; others he was disoriented and weak. Sometimes he was affectionate, others he was angry. This is the way it is with the terminally ill—"peaks and valleys," a family friend who had lost her son to brain cancer that summer told me, though on the peaks it was hard to believe we were only enroute to the next valley. Officially there was nothing wrong with him. The doctor had ruled out cancer and still insisted he didn't have TB. Only gradually did we understand that he was dying. We were novices at death. The first time my father-in-law had to urinate when I was alone with him, I was clumsy with shyness and didn't fit the urinal tightly enough to his groin; he peed all over himself and the bed. That didn't seem like a peak, but it was—he was alert enough to be irked with me.

His medications flavored everything, and Koke complained of the taste they left in his mouth. Even water tasted salty (though later, when he clamored for a beer and we gave him water, telling him it was beer, he pronounced it "Dee-licious!"). He had no appetite; the drugs made him queasy, and so an antinausea was added to the mix. When the staff asked if there was anything he would eat, he requested spaghetti and meatballs with garlic bread, but when they came he barely touched them, and by the next time they tried to tempt him, his food was being pureed, and his spaghetti and meatballs were just a nasty-looking scoop of mush on his plate.

The staff was extraordinarily kind, and if I have no recollection of smell, it is because Westminster's Health Care did not smell even faintly of disinfectant, feces, or urine, those stenches that linger in the hallways of so many nursing homes, nor did it smell of fresh air, for on that corridor of invalids we were as sealed from the rest of the world as the patients. We were steps from Chesapeake Bay but scarcely saw it. That November was unseasonably balmy, though my only memory of the weather is passing through the courtyard on our way from the motel each morning, through the clanging steel gate, past the goldfish in the fountain, to the automatic sliding glass doors that seemed to suck us inside, into the quiet, steady hum of the filtered, odorless air that became our season, for though we had to keep meeting our classes, driving back and forth, only the second floor of Westminster's Health Care, especially its sounds—the carpet-muffled clatter of the nurse's cart, the shifting of trays, the swing of the heavy doors, the footsteps and voices of the aides, most of all the voices of the other patients, so noticeable for the way they stirred the muted tranquility—seemed to register.

From one side we heard the cranky muttering of Mr. Crocker. Once as I sat on the hallway sofa outside his room an aide gasped as she entered. "You need to put some pants on!" she commanded. "That's a good idea," Mr. Crocker said, then, lest he seem too obliging, "Don't put them there!" As she left, she rolled her eyes at the aide coming in to shave him and said, "Good luck in there, Sharon."

Across the hall was Mrs. Barnes, who wandered the corridor day and night, wearing white nylon knee-highs with a hiked up skirt and cockeyed wig. Occasionally she wandered into Koke's room, and one night we heard the crash of a tray and the exasperated voice of a substitute aide cry out, "Get back, Mrs. Barnes! Go to bed!"

All day every day we heard Mr. Cathey, the Redskins fan in the room next door. Passing his room, we glimpsed the maroon and gold Redskins blanket covering his bed, the helmet lamp and wastebasket and pennants, along with the bobble-headed Redskins doll that played the theme to "Monday Night Football" very loud. Van Halen and Fleetwood Mac were even louder, but no matter how often the aides admonished him to turn down his music, he forgot. His own voice boomed through the wall several times a day. "Ow-ow-ow-ow-ow," he shouted. "Goddamn! Goddamn!" When I asked an aide what was wrong with him, thinking he might have Tourette's, she smiled and said, "Mr. Cathey is very tight." He was brain-damaged, she confided, and his family simply adored him.

But my father-in-law was the staff's favorite, or so they let us believe. "Mr. Gaspeny," they would call softly to get his attention when they came into the room. "Mr. Gaspeny," he repeated to me. "I just need my light turned on. I can't see it."

He began to talk about light. He was having TIA after TIA. His doctor, who had taken him off Coumadin, refused to permit even the baby aspirin my sister-in-law suggested, and the small strokes had begun to wrench his body. When Michael and I tried to wheel him out to the Bay for what would prove his last ride, his legs had acquired such an iron drift that even a board tied across the footrests couldn't keep his right foot from wedging between them and dragging on the ground.

Still there were good moments. When I reported that he'd been flirting with the aides, he smiled and admitted, "I probably have." After one hard morning, he'd had some lucid time while Michael was at lunch, and I told him his friend Ken Beck had come to pray for the Lord to give him breath. When I noted that his breathing had immediately calmed and he'd fallen asleep, adding, "Pretty powerful prayer, huh?" he laughed and said, "You're beautiful."

"I don't know what I want to do," he said. "I want to follow the cycle of my thoughts." Later, "I want to get up and do something, but I don't know what it is."

Initially what he wanted was to do things for himself. When an aide came in to shave the little patch of skin between his sideburns and goatee, he pitched a fit, afraid she would cut his sideburns too short. I had been brushing his teeth and cleaning his partial, but when he decided he wanted to do that too, I brought the brush and paste, a basin, a glass, and the mirror to his bedside tray and watched as slowly, so slowly, he raised a trembling hand, paused, and then reached out to brush the teeth inside the mirror.

"I am trying to clear my throat," he said. "I am trying to drink some cold water. Just watch me."

It was all we could do, watch.

"I feel weird," he said, complaining that he had "ducks" on his back. "I will pour it in. I just need a drink of cold water."

His skin was dry no matter how much lotion we applied. It kept tearing, and his arms were covered with patches of gauze. Once he asked me to look at a scab of blood on the lambskin that covered his sheet. "I must have gone to the bathroom," he said. When I told him it was blood, he gave me a wary look. "It looks like fecal matter," he said.

"I am beginning to see the light," he said. "I may have one." Then, "I have one."

After an especially rough Saturday, on which he was angry, frightened, and extremely weak, though it took all our strength to keep his legs in the bed, he was given morphine for the first time. The next day when Michael bent over the urinal, Koke smiled as he reached out to pat his son's head. Later, when I wasn't there—for so many of our experiences were solitary as we covered each other for meals, a little bit of exercise, and the papers we couldn't concentrate on grading—he said, "I haven't been very nice to you, Michael." Had I been present, I might have protested—he'd always been wonderful to us—but it was exactly the acknowledgement Michael wanted.

He was walking, he told us, and in the bed his legs churned. He was walking on a pier, watching the men catch fish. "What kind of fish?" I asked, and he gave me a beatific smile. "A lot of fish," then, after a pause, "Lots of beautiful fish." He had caught permit, pompano, grouper, tarpon, bonefish, snook, sea trout, porgy, grunts, sheepshead, snappers. He knew all their names; his son was a fisherman. He knew the names of all the trees and birds in the Keys; when you walked with him in North Carolina, he would point out the sweet Betsy, the beautyberry, spicebush, japonica. "What color are they?" I pressed, and he smiled again. "Silver. Lots of silver fish." And I could see them, could see the concrete pier so clean and white in the morning sun, the lustrous blue sky overhead and below the blue-blue-green of the ocean, from which fishermen clad in bright red shirts were pulling fish after glistening silver-white fish.

No longer did we leave the room when aides came to bathe him. Standing naked on the bed, he announced, "I'm having my testicles washed," with the same tickled pride with which he would later announce, "I have just taken a shit," though in fact he hadn't taken a shit in more than thirty years. Was he wandering his childhood? "I was right," he said. "The bag next to me seems to be holding on."

He tried to tell us where he was. "I'm walking someplace strange. I'm climbing stairs. I'm climbing the stairs." We held our breaths. "I'm at the top of the stairs. I see the light." This was it, our own private tour of death. "I see it," he said. "I see the blue light." Our eyes widened as we looked at each other and clapped our hands to our mouths to stifle the laughter bubbling in our throats. What if the heavens parted, and all you saw was a Kmart Blue Light Special?

"I can see me now running under the truck." Or did he say *track*?

"I am getting old, and I cannot do these things I want to do." Sometimes he sounded resigned, but often he grew agitated. "Nobody believes me," he kept moaning, his voice wrenching with despair. "I'm trying to tell you...." But when we asked what he was trying to tell us, he grew angry. "I'm trying to tell you," he repeated, weeping.

"Will you help me get up?"

Should we have acknowledged that he was dying? "I am nearing the end of my journey," he said, and I promised, "We're not going to let you go alone." It was as close as I could come. "We'll be with you."

"All right," he said. But later he wept again. "Nobody understands," he wailed, and then with a loud and terrible flatness, "I am going to be dead."

From next door came the *Monday Night Football* theme. *Ow-ow-ow-ow-ow. Goddamn.*

Get back, Mrs. Barnes, an aide shouted. *Go to bed, Mrs. Barnes.*

Good luck in there, Sharon.

When my father-in-law could no longer swallow, we swabbed his mouth, but he bit the swab, and we were afraid he would choke; so we dabbed his cracked lips. His last word was *water*. And when he could no longer make the sound, water was the last shape of a word on his lips. "He can hear you," the nurse promised as she instructed us to say goodbye. But I couldn't, and I told him so. Instead I said, "Let's just say I'll see you again."

He could no longer close his eyes, and I don't know if he slept. Still he held on, and when I asked the nurse how long, she shook her head. "You have to labor to die just like you labor to give birth," she explained. I was dumbstruck. I knew what it was like to labor to give birth, but why should we have to labor to die? My father-in-law had always made death sound as casual as an errand, but that was when he thought he'd be willing to go. The agony of Félicité, Flaubert's simple heart, shook her sides; Tolstoy's Ivan Ilyich screamed for three days; but until my father-in-law lay dying I had thought death's labors the stuff of nineteenth-century novels. I should have known what a struggle it is for the body to defeat the mind.

Max came for Thanksgiving, and I told Koke we were together just as I'd said. All morning of the Saturday after Thanksgiving, before he had to return to college, Max held Koke's hand. My father-in-law's labor began late that afternoon. His breath caught, then rattled so loudly it seemed as if it might shatter his chest before it subsided into a rasping pant that seemed to go on and on until his breath just stopped. Each time we bent our heads to his chest in time to hear it catch and begin its rattle again. Over and over. At midnight the nurse told us to go home. "You're exhausted," she said. "You need to get some sleep." She promised she would call if there was any change.

She called at 4:30 a.m. "He wasn't going to die in front of you," she said.

4

MY FATHER-IN-LAW always said that a smile and a pair of well-shined shoes would open any door. So Michael polished his shoes, I fetched his Frank Nitti suit from the closet, and at the viewing Michael tucked a notebook and a pencil in its pocket. We buried him in a graveside service with three eulogies and full military honors.

His doctor was wrong. He died of tuberculosis. In the old days they called it consumption, which seems an apt name.

But when I remember my father-in-law in that month he was dying, I don't think about the roughness of the passage or how he balked and raged at the end. Instead I see him in his hospital bed in Westminster, walking someplace strange, he reports, his legs pitching beneath the sheet as he tries to balance on the deck of the ferry. He tried to tell us where he was going, but I didn't want him to go, I didn't want him to leave us. And so I called, loud enough to be heard above the angry current, "Koke! Koke, what did Harry have?" He was no longer with us, already more than halfway across, but he sat straight up in the bed, grinned, and said, "Haarrry had *prin-ci-ples*." And I'll be damned if we didn't laugh until we cried.

Inside the Palace

THOMAS STEWART HILLMER
September 15, 1956–April 14, 2005

THE BLUE HYDRANGEA I planted on the morning I learned of your death has bloomed again. It has flourished in its spot beside the entrance to the vegetable garden, larger now than the older pink hydrangeas there along the cedar fence in the shade where the small pond used to be. The shade has thickened beneath the steep flank of the new two-story garage next door, and perhaps I should transplant them, though I always thought hydrangeas liked a bit of shade and a fence or wall for shelter. It's the sort of thing I once might have discussed with you, and so it seems fitting that I was in the garden when Mike stepped outside the back door to deliver your sad news. Though it had been cool much of the week, that morning was warm and sunny, the kind of balmy April Saturday that draws me to the garden with a hunger that can be filled only by the crumbling of dirt beneath my trowel and tug of tender white webs of roots clinging to their plastic nursery pots. Had I thought of you that morning, as I tamped the hydrangea into place and began to set out the annuals, the gaudy melampodium, my favorite clown-faced torenia (the wishbone flower—isn't that a lovely name?), red pentas for the hummingbirds, I would have imagined you in your garden, perhaps giving the compost barrel you built one last rotation before amending the soil where you would soon plant tomatoes or weeding around your delicate heads of buttercrunch lettuce. You were proud of that barrel; you were proud of your garden, which was perfect—it had to be, or you would grow angry and rip it out. You were that way. But a garden in spring is the purest kind of hope. Late each winter you would start seeds in flats in the small room off your kitchen, okra, green beans, for me impatiens the color of apricots. How well I remember the spring vegetables you used to bring us, along with the big round loaves of potato bread you baked all year, such a favorite in our house we called it Tom Bread. It was summer the last time I saw your garden, though I can't say what year, only that it was more than a year before you died, maybe two or even three. You demonstrated the compost barrel, and I admired the precise green rows of tomato plants and peppers, fringed along one side with cosmos, bright flags of pink, magenta, and white. So pretty. I don't know when you made your decision, but I think it must have been final, there would have been no going back, when you chose that spring not to plant a garden.

I'm sure Michael said, "There's some bad news." His face wore a bewildered look of shock, and as he cut across the lawn I rose from my plot of dirt to meet him. Your obituary had run in the morning paper, but both of us had missed it. Our friend Ansley had noticed it and called. I hate that my first words were "Was it a suicide?" But those would have been the first words of anyone who knew you. I don't mean I wasn't stunned, only that we had always seen that cloud on a far horizon, though the distance between you and it had narrowed in the last years, which explains why I can't say when I last saw you. It was hard to be around you.

Fourteen years before it had been your brother Warren. You seemed resigned to his death, though once, a few years later, speaking of him to us, you broke down and sobbed, a howl of grief that was as much for his despair as for his dying. After his death you hung a small framed black-and-white picture of the two of you as little boys in cowboy suits on your bedroom wall, the same wall that held Arnold Doren's photograph of a green-eyed Italian child, which you bought as a gift for your sister Sarah, though you loved the image so much she insisted you share it. There were paintings in your living room—one of Sarah's, a fish by your friend Terry—but the only other picture I recall in your bedroom was a small matted photograph of two oystercatchers at Ocracoke that I gave you because you liked birds. I intended to give you one of the landscape miniatures I was working on in Polaroid transfer, a beach scene because you loved Pawleys Island so much, but Pawleys was also the locus of so many painful family memories that I decided not to, though now that I know you visited by yourself that spring one last time to say goodbye, I wish that I had.

I think it was your obsession with detail that gave you a taste for small things. When I went to the Grand Canyon, I brought you a little burro carved of stone and a painted Acoma clay turtle no larger than a quarter for the collection of tiny animals on top of the bookcase you built for your living room. You were always so grateful for the least gifts, a tee shirt I bought for you at the Japanese Garden in Golden Gate Park, a postcard, a piece of my oregano plant, even my decent used potholders. I suspect you lived so frugally less by inclination than by choice—it was the price of working part-time. More than money, more than things, you wanted hours, for your garden, reading, tennis, long walks, and of course for your projects. You always had a project. The birdhouse you made for us still hangs on our back fence; over the years it has sheltered chickadees, titmice, wrens. Bluebirds nest in the houses you constructed for the Audubon Society along Buffalo Creek. Once you threw a party for John Cheever's birthday, baked a Lady Baltimore cake, assigned your guests readings, and built a lectern that later became your dictionary stand. They worked in concert, your hands and habits of mind. You loved books, and though your library wasn't huge, you owned the entire set of Patrick O'Brian's Aubrey/Maturin series in hardback, including, I'm sure, the unfinished novel published six months before you died. You and Mike created a Flaubertian Society with a membership of two. When your biology professor found "It's no real pleasure in life" scrawled on the chalkboard of his classroom and demanded that students identify what was wrong with the sentence, you said, "Nothing. It's the last line of Flannery O'Connor's 'A Good Man Is Hard to Find.'" You laughed when you reported that he told you he didn't care who wrote it, bad grammar was bad grammar, but bitterness curdled beneath your smile. You loved O'Connor's black humor. You loved irony in all its forms until you were lost and saw only blackness with no humor or irony at all. And though you loved everything you loved without condition, you wanted credit. It was the secret pain inside your attraction to all things ironic; it was why you loved Cheever. Every year you and Mike reread *Falconer*, laughing out loud. But the book your heart always returned to was William Maxwell's beautiful novella, *So Long, See You Tomorrow*. You were drawn to its elegiac sadness, its eloquent truths about memory's lies and desires, and you kept a picture of the Giacometti sculpture that haunts the narrator with its suggestion that we might walk through the walls of time, "The Palace at 4 a.m.," folded inside your copy. You chose your books like cherished companions, and when Sarah sold them to a used bookstore after your death—something that distressed Mike, who knew your library so well it grieved him not to be able to go through those books one last time—Jim Clark bought your copy of *Helping Muriel Make It Through the Night* to return to me, but when I opened it to read the inscription, I discovered that you had never asked me to sign it. I don't know what I hoped—that in the absence of any message from you I might have found one in my words to you? It makes no sense, but there it is, that wish for some trace of recognition in a book that shows no sign of ever having passed through your hands at all.

And so I go through those things I remember in your hands instead, all those objects now scattered and gone, important to you in the way that possessions often are for people who don't have many: the mismatched pots and pans hanging on the pegboard in your kitchen, your white ironstone plates, the same dime-store pattern I used in grad school, your nubby brown placemats. I take my seat at the card table you set up for us in the living room, and as I unfold my napkin, laundered soft, faded to the color of weak mulberry tea, it occurs to me to wonder where you sat to eat by yourself every night. Whatever meal you have fixed, you would have worried and fussed, though you needn't have. We clear the dishes, and as you run water in the sink I lean against your counter, the wood surface you refinished smooth as glass to the touch. You are relaxed now, I hope. The food was delicious; the evening is a success. We are here among your things in your kitchen.

Clothes gave you pleasure. I remember you best in a brown wool sweater with a moth hole in the sleeve, and more often in khakis than jeans. Yours was a threadbare aristocracy, a shabby genteel L.L. Bean look. You liked flannel shirts, and every Christmas one of the women who worked with you at the hospital pharmacy gave you a new one. Once, for a friend's wedding, you splurged on a Brooks Brothers suit, along with shirt, tie, socks, and dress shoes. The suit made you so happy I took a picture of you in it, though, typical of you, you decided not to attend the wedding after all and later joked that the only occasions you wore it to were funerals.

You bought a TV and kept it in a box in your closet because otherwise you would be tempted to watch it. And joked about that too. You loved *The Andy Griffith Show* and *M*A*S*H*, and at the pharmacy you requested the early dinner hour so you could watch reruns in the break room; at bars you would attempt to switch off the ball game when it was time for Opie, Andy, and Aunt Bee. You delighted in the naughty ironies of *M*A*S*H*, but it was the sweet innocence of Mayberry you craved, and in the last years, after your father's death, when you were restoring your mother's ancestral home in Cameron, the beautiful two-story white frame house with wraparound porches and gingerbread trim that you blamed her for allowing to fall into disrepair, you spent more and more time in that small Sandhills town where you would die, a town that looks less like a town than a collector's display, a village of antique shops and handsome old houses strung like pearls along a short stretch of country highway, a toy town, population 151, a wish, less a holdover from the past than a desire for it, a longing for memory you must have recognized, for despite the anguish that house held for you, despite the many times you quit therapy because it was just too painful to dredge up the past, you were surely seeking some image of lost happiness, no matter how brief. You too longed to walk through the walls of time.

Yesterday I felt as if I might have walked through those walls too, for when I drove past your apartment on Cedar Street, there was a bike that could have been yours parked on your porch, nothing fancy, just an old three-speed, a way to get around, cheaper and more reliable than the used green Chevette your father gave you. Later Warren's brown Volvo wagon replaced the balky Chevette. You mourned Warren's death but came up in the world. His plaid sofa relegated the metal glider you'd used for a living room couch to the porch, and in your bedroom the matching loveseat held neat stacks of shirts. I wonder what you would make of the new central air units outside your bedroom window. Would you have welcomed the relief from the summer heat or protested a hike in rent? I can hear your complaints—the rumble of the fan just beyond the wall alongside your bed, the displacement of your bird feeder, or maybe it would be the thermostat that didn't work right. The sight of the parking lot for new condos on your corner would infuriate you every time you passed, and the new ballpark would have put you in such a state—the noise, the lights, the traffic, the people cutting through the Cedar Street yards en route from their remote parking—that every now and then Mike and I remark ruefully to each other it's a good thing you died before it opened. You lived in that apartment so many years that long before your death you developed the spleen of an old codger, loathing each new neighbor and every change to the street. The kitten upstairs sent you into a rage; you couldn't stand the "stupid" owner or the hours he kept. You wanted everything to stay the way it had been, back in the days when your dog Betsy was still alive and your friend TM's old girlfriend Beth lived next door and the three of you would do things together. I think that was one of your happiest times, though even at your happiest resentment festered inside you. But Betsy died, Beth finished her degree and moved out of town, and you were leaving yourself, for veterinary school at North Carolina State.

We were thrilled when you seemed to turn school around, the same way you once turned your tendency to get stumbling drunk around. Your academic record was spotty. Before we met, you had flunked out of East Carolina. It must have been soon after that you came to Greensboro, where your sister Sarah was an art student at UNCG, or perhaps she was already managing the GreenHill Gallery. For years, long after Sarah moved to New York, you attended classes part-time, dropping one after another because you weren't certain you would make an A on the upcoming exam. You were the perfectionist who would rather walk away or fail than achieve anything less than impeccable. It seemed miraculous when you settled on vet school and determined to get your B.S. You came so close. If Betsy hadn't been killed—*Tom, Tom,* I still want to say, *why didn't you use a leash?* You couldn't finish your last semester. You began working on a scientific theory, something to do with the brain having evolved out of the stomach—Betsy had come back from the dead to tell you, you said, it was her gift to you. You were doing research, you were writing, you were proving the case, the missing link between the human brain and the stomach that was going to turn the science word upside down, people would take note, we would see, you sat in our living room and told us, and there was no humor, no irony now, you were manic, you had a lot of work to do, but it was worth it, Betsy's last gift, the Nobel Prize. All that late spring and summer TM, Beth, Mike, and I worried and conferred. You were failing your classes, in the fall you would go off to Raleigh without telling State you hadn't graduated, but there was no doubt in your mind—because it was not just grief that drove you mad but guilt, and only the whole world's applause would have been enough to assuage it—you were going to win the Nobel Prize.

When you left in the fall I suppose we hoped the new environment would heal you, but you hated the trailer your father bought for you in Cary, hated Cary, then hated even more that you had to keep living there after you dropped out of State your first semester. The program was much too competitive for anyone as fragile as you, especially that year. Such cruel timing, that car out of nowhere, the dog lunging into the street. After your death TM told me he thought you'd lost your one chance for happiness then, though truth be told I'm not sure you ever had one.

I don't remember how long you lived in Cary, only that you moved to Chapel Hill for a while after you left, but you hated Chapel Hill too, it was full of snobs, you said, you couldn't make a friend, and you leapt at the chance to move back to Greensboro when the apartment above your old rooms on Cedar Street came vacant. I was surprised when you gave that aerie up to move back downstairs; it had such a lovely front porch balcony in the treetops where you once served us dinner, but you missed the easy access to the backyard, and I suppose reclaiming your old apartment felt like coming home.

That handsome boy, my mother always called you, and you were. A twinkle lit your brown eyes despite your tendency to depression. With your classic features, your tanned skin, and hair the color and sheen of rich coffee, you were much too handsome to be so unsuccessful with women. Mike remembers a girl named Rose who broke your heart before we met you. Later there was Coppie, who cared about you for the rest of your life—two weeks after you died she called me, hysterical, having found your obituary in a stack of papers she was taking to the recycling bin—but somehow the relationship dwindled into a friendship, and later she married the professor from Alaska and for a while lived up there. After that there was a brief affair with D's crazy girlfriend. But there weren't many women in your life. Several years later, when you had a crush on a young woman who worked at the hospital and asked if I thought you should ask her out, I said, "Of course." But when she told you she had a boyfriend, you felt so humiliated I don't think you ever attempted another romantic interaction.

Am I telling you things you already know? How could I be? I'm telling you what I remember. You're the one who chose to forget everything.

I think we must have met you in the summer of 1979. The first time you appear on my calendar is August 4 of that year; we played pool with you and D, again the next night, and a few days later. Whatever the season, we met you one night at the Pickwick through D, who had been my student and was for a short time your sister Sarah's boyfriend. D was drunk by the time Sarah came in, and I still remember the soft fondness of her sigh as she said, "Oh dear. I haven't done a very good job of looking out for you tonight." She and D soon parted, but you and D are all over my calendar that fall, including one night in October when my mother was visiting from the Midwest and the two of you, Ansley and Martha, Roy and Andrea dropped in, and we all played poker.

D got my mother drunk, and she had a wonderful time, though it was you, not D, that she remembered ever after, that handsome boy. She took a picture of us around the table. It's hard to look at that picture now, all of us so young and happy as we inspect our hands for luck, now that you and Martha are both suicides, and Roy is surely dead—the last I heard after he and Andrea divorced, he was in New Orleans hoping for a liver transplant. And Ansley too is gone, lost to renal failure in 2011. When I do look, what I see is the wall behind us, my collection of antique photographs, sepia and brown, all those stern faces, those pictures within the picture, such a muted backdrop for our vibrant skin and bright clothes, a cautionary Capuchin Crypt, those portraits of the already dead I've hung just behind our shoulders.

Going through those old calendars, I'm surprised by how little I wrote on them back then. I was too young to know how much we forget, and so I find first names with no last names and haven't a clue, events I might as well not have attended, places I would swear I've never been, at the same time I stumble upon a single word that brings back time and place with such clarity it's astonishing to realize that without that prompt I would not recall them at all. 1980, Palm Sunday and Easter both: dinner at D and Tom's. I had forgotten you and D briefly shared quarters and no longer remember where they were, yet suddenly there I am again in the kitchen of some second-floor apartment, address unknown, standing at the old-fashioned sink in a wash of white light, peeler in hand, making potatoes au gratin.

Later that year Mike and I moved to Princeton. When we came back you no longer appeared on my calendars so frequently, for those were the seasons when you and D, then later only you, were often just the extra plates at our table, those impromptu suppers that went unrecorded, and so it's impossible to reconstruct just how often we saw you. You helped us move from the little house on Hill Street where we lived when we met you to the big Dutch Colonial we still occupy, and at the end of the day we all crowded around the breakfast room table and ate gumbo. You spent much of that summer here, hanging ceiling fans, repairing our vintage 1924 plumbing, washing windows, patching plaster. Your fussing drove us crazy, but you're in every room; I look out the bay window in back and see you hosing off the storm windows you've propped against the big maple lost to a storm years ago now, a white tee shirt wrapped around your head like a keffiyeh. In those days I gave a lot of parties for visiting writers, and you would have been at them all, though I kept no lists of guests. Pool at Logan's, darts at the Camelot. Later, after Mike and I had our son Max, we became less spontaneous, less flexible, something people without children never understand. Only a few nights before he was born we went to see *Sophie's Choice* with you and had dinner at the Far East, where you always ordered moo shu pork; it would be the last evening we all went to dinner and a movie for a long time.

But you welcomed him. "Gee, most babies are ugly, but he's kind of cute," you said when you came to see me in the hospital, bearing a brick of disposable diapers. You and Mike were in the habit of having coffee at your apartment every Saturday, and once Max was weaned Mike began to bring him along. You fed him the store-brand fig cakes you preferred to Fig Newtons, and it was from you he learned to say, "More fig cake please." I have a picture of him sitting on your lap in your backyard, his plump baby hand waving one of those half-eaten cookies. But then you got Betsy. He was afraid of her, having been bitten by one of his own dogs when he was ten months old, and the Saturday morning ritual of Folgers and fig cakes tapered off. Max doesn't remember any of that, of course, but he does remember fishing with you and D at a pond off Route 70. He remembers playing softball with you and Mike. You were there the day he was sent to retrieve a foul ball and was arrested by the sight of a hawk swooping down for a squirrel while one of my colleagues kept screaming, "Where's the ball? Bring back the ball!" You were there the day the same colleague borrowed Max's sacred Orioles cap and ruined it, and if you were not beyond memory now, you would probably recall that he promised to replace it but never did. You couldn't stand the professors who played on that team. You thought they were snobs. After all, some of them had failed you.

Once the four of us drove to an exhibit of contemporary British painting at the Southeastern Center for Contemporary

Art in Winston-Salem, and when I pointed out a particularly ugly church on Silas Creek Parkway, you said dryly, "I wouldn't want to *worship* there." It was the way you said worship that cracked me up; I've never passed that church since without thinking of you and laughing. We laughed a lot back then, and I can still hear the exact pitch of amusement that seeped into your droll chuckle. Sometimes we had you over for dinner and a movie on the VCR, but as our career and family obligations grew more complex, the dinners grew fewer and more formal. You fretted over your menus months in advance, then worried till next time whether the food had been right. I took to jotting mine down, perhaps because I knew how you looked forward to those evenings and wanted to make them special; so much time would pass between, I didn't want to repeat myself by accident. Chilled sorrel soup, baby greens with Kalamata olives, hearts of palm, and tomatoes from our garden, grilled filet mignon, sautéed mushrooms, rosemary roast potatoes, Vichy carrots, blackberry cobbler. Seared tuna steaks with a lemony mustard caper sauce. Glazed veal chops. Orzo with saffron, rice with scallions and pecans, roasted asparagus, corn pudding, a sauté of zucchini and red peppers. Apple cake, Viennese brownies, pecan pie.

It was a flashback to the spontaneity of the old days when the mother of one of Max's friends gave us three tickets to the Paul Simon/Bob Dylan concert in Raleigh at the last minute and we called to see if you wanted to go. Our own little Woodstock thirty years late—we brought beach chairs and sat on the Walnut Creek lawn in the rain, digging every minute. How you laughed when I came back from the ladies' room at intermission and reported the earnestness with which the grandmother in front of me in line had confided to her friend that she just wished she could meet Bob, because her daughter had named her son Dylan in his honor and she thought it would make him so happy to know that. Five years after you died, programming my iPod for the hour-and-fifteen-minute drive to Cameron to visit your grave, I thought of that night again and played Dylan all the way down, Paul Simon all the way back, and for weeks I couldn't get "Crazy Love" and "I Know What I Know" out of my head.

It was the first time I'd gone since the evening of your service, and I didn't remember Cameron at all, the directions Mike got from the church having brought us in from the other side; we saw only the gables of your mother's house through the trees as we came over the overpass and then, a few yards up on the other side the pretty white-frame Presbyterian church with the Cameron cemetery behind. We were early, and so we strolled the sandy lane among the pines into a field of wildflowers. (Half a decade later when I walked the same lane, I turned the other way and surprised a meadow full of chickens and goats.) By the time we got back to the church the women from the pharmacy had arrived, and we sat together at the picnic table outside. Only the weekend before, they said, you had come into work feigning jet lag, complaining you were exhausted from the wedding, and when they asked who got married, you told them Prince Charles and Camilla Parker Bowles. They loved that, loved the way you teased them and made them laugh, and they raved about your baking. "He even made the crust from scratch!" they said of a lemon meringue pie you had brought in for a co-worker's birthday. Mike and I mentioned that we felt the most appropriate memorial would be to have the trail you cleared for the Audubon Society in the wooded area behind the hospital named for you; they suggested placing something like a birdbath there in your honor. When it was nearly time for the service, one by one we went upstairs to the ladies' room in the education building the church had left open. There was something in its tidiness that brought your bathroom back to me, the clean, faded towels I would never dry my hands on again, so neatly folded on your rack. It is always the mundane detail, that smallest of vessels, that contains most acutely the enormity of loss.

I don't recall the service, only that as soon as we took our seats in the folding chairs at the family plot, where your father's and Warren's ashes lay beneath their flat pink granite stones, your family filed in, your three sisters and remaining brother. Your mother wasn't there. I thought she must be too frail to come. Five years later I was surprised to see that she had not yet joined you in that place where so many of her family are buried, such a peaceful, shady precinct for eternity, no chain-link fences, encroaching businesses, or highway noise to disturb its population's slumber, only Cameron's picture-perfect churches and houses and the woods beyond. There's a magnolia tree near your grave, along with a mimosa and a couple of tall pines. You seemed at home there, you've settled in; I was the one not used to the neighborhood, and the sight of your name on the stone made me cry, at the same time there was comfort in it too, so much more bearable a last image than the black metal box resting on the folding table that had been placed in front of the family plot for the service. It looked like an oversized recipe tin, a file of notes to be tossed as soon as the term paper was graded, fitting casket for no one, least of all anyone with your sense of aesthetics. If you had still been you, you would have snorted and said, "I wouldn't want to rest there."

Terry had driven up from Charlotte. You must have left his address for Sarah, for when we spoke to her after the service she promised to return his painting. She was coming to Greensboro later that week to clean out your apartment, and she said simply that she expected to find it very orderly, paused, then repeated herself as if to make sure we understood her meaning, the only confirmation we would have for what we all knew. It was Terry who told us you had visited Pawleys Island by yourself that spring. That may have been where you were when you pretended to have flown to London for Prince Charles's wedding.

It was a perfect spring evening, scented with wisteria and warming earth, a pearly gray light anticipating the coming dusk, so unlike the steep gloom of the August afternoon when I drove back to see your grave, windshield wipers on and off against an intermittent drizzle, an afternoon so unpleasantly hot and humid gnats made it hard to linger. I hadn't decided to come until the last minute, and I felt sticky and dirty in cropped dungarees. A bright silk petal lay on the ground near your grave, blown from an arrangement in one of the nearby urns. I hadn't thought to bring a flower, and so I retraced the walk Mike and I had taken into the field, but the season of wildflowers was past; all I could find was a small yellow hawkweed. I brushed away a few pine needles and placed it on your stone before I spotted the brilliant red and yellow lantana growing atop the mounded breast of a grave across the lane. I could have brought lantana from my own garden if I'd planned. I thought of the brick of diapers you'd given me when Max was born, pinched from the hospital pharmacy no doubt, and swiped a single blossom from your neighbor, which I lay beside the hawkweed, then drove back to Greensboro, doing my best not to weep as I sang along with Paul Simon.

The last time you appear on my calendar is an October evening two and a half years before your death, on the trail you cleared for the Audubon Society. You gave us a tour, pointing out the places where you had seen a screech owl, a green heron, or a red-shouldered hawk. Afterwards you served beer, wine, and hors d'oeuvres at the picnic table by the trailhead, and we went back to your apartment for dinner. You were pleased by your work, though you had harsh words for some of the members of the Audubon Society who'd helped—it was *your* trail, just as Cedar Street was your street, and you didn't want to share it with anyone whose ambitions differed from yours. In the two years since your father's death your complaints had grown sharper, more frequent, more misanthropic. We had deceived ourselves when you moved back from Chapel Hill and Cary; you'd seemed happier, as if coming home had given you some measure of peace, but gradually all the old anger about past slights and failures returned, accompanied by a growing list of new ones. After your death TM remembered that on his last visit you'd proudly shown him a fishing rod case you'd made for a relative who'd loaned you gear for a trip, then in the next breath complained that the recipient probably wouldn't appreciate it. He felt it summed up your tortured view of the world. I think all you ever really wanted was to be recognized; yet no recognition sufficed. Even on the lovely evening you guided us along the Audubon trail your bitterness was overwhelming, and one of the last times Mike saw you, sometime in the last year of your life, when the two of you took in a ball game, you could speak of nothing else, until the expression on Mike's face caused you to blurt, "I'm bumming you out, aren't I?" I grew to dread your voice on the phone, so abrupt and harsh with disuse it lost all inflection. "Are you doing all right?" you would ask, but it wasn't a question, it wasn't even a voice, just a sandpaper rasp, the bark and scrape of a hinge covered in rust.

The trail is named for you now. I wish I could tell you that was my doing. When my emails to the Audubon Society went unanswered in the months after your death, you would not have been surprised. The silence would have confirmed your sour expectations, the rage I suspect you held on to because in the end it was the only thing you felt you truly possessed. For a while I persisted, then let it go. Someone more tenacious must have had the idea too, perhaps the women at the pharmacy or the very people you complained of the night you served us hors d'oeuvres at the trailhead. Mike stumbled upon the sign on one of his long walks a few springs ago. Online I found a back issue of the local Society newsletter with a notice of the trail's dedication. Drainage work along the creek had caused a three-year delay. But there you are, recognized at last, your name spelled correctly (how it used to irritate you when people left off the second *l*), though when I tried to walk the trail I had to circle the area several times in search of parking—there are no longer any spaces along the street where we parked that night, and without that convenience the trail was so overgrown I had to turn back.

The last time you had dinner at our house was in the summer of 2000. Your father had died the year before, and you were preoccupied with the restoration of your mother's house. Looking back, I remember the resentment with which you spoke of her and your need to stay on top of the workmen, and realize it must have been your father's death that brought on that last downward spiral. I wouldn't have thought so at the time, for my memory of your father was the story you told about the exacting Army captain who filled in the family swimming pool because one of the kids had peed in it, told with a dry chuckle, oblivious to my horror, just as I was oblivious to the fact that you loved him. You claimed to hate your mother and one of your sisters; you and Sarah, once so close, had a falling out; but you loved your father. You couldn't please him, but he could make you laugh. We ate on the deck, and at some point that evening we inspected the site where I intended to put in a pond. A microburst had claimed the big maple in our backyard two months before, a storm so severe all the tree companies were backlogged and I was still waiting for the stump to be ground out. A month later, when the pond was in place, you brought me rocks from the Tennessee River for the waterfall. I no longer remember how you came to have them, only that, born on Signal Mountain, you were a fan of all things Tennessee. They're still there, though I could no longer tell you which ones they are.

I've said you seemed more relaxed when you came back from Raleigh and Chapel Hill, and you did. At least there was no more talk about the brain and the stomach, no more travel to Stockholm in your Brooks Brothers suit. You had a new project. You were preoccupied with F. Scott Fitzgerald's *Tender is the Night*, a new theory that would revolutionize Fitzgerald scholarship, and we didn't have the heart to tell you that we saw you acting out your envy of your friend Chad, who had left Greensboro for another university, where he was writing a dissertation on *Tender is the Night*. No doubt you were trying to win back his friendship too. You loved him as much as you resented him; I think you considered him the closest friend you ever had. When he and his wife came back for a visit after they first moved, you gave them a party. You were in your element that night, but as their family expanded you complained that his wife resented your visits and tried to shield him from you. Perhaps she did; I can't say. In any case, I think you worked on Fitzgerald until your father got sick.

When you died I emailed Chad and TM. By that time Chad was a college administrator, TM the director of a writing center at a university. All that summer TM and I grieved together in cyberspace. "It's odd," he wrote to me at one point, "the things that stick in your mind. For me, it's the image of Tom's suntanned hands shaking out wet lettuce in his kitchen sink with short, methodical snaps. The boy was meticulous, eh." Chad sent a brief reply, thanking me for the information, in which he never mentioned your name.

When do you know for certain that someone is lost? For Mike it was the autumn before you died, when he took our Labrador puppy over to meet you, and you who loved dogs so much showed no interest. For years we'd encouraged you to get another dog, but you refused, saying the same thing would just happen again. Buy a house, we said; you're so handy it would be nothing for you to fence in the yard. And for a while you looked. But you couldn't find an affordable house that you liked, and when you thought you might like the house, then you were certain you wouldn't like the neighbors. In your last summer you chose a house on Cedar Street, but Sarah wouldn't release the money from your father's estate for the down payment, or at least that's what we heard. Would it have made a difference? The moment I knew you were lost was the last time I saw your apartment, possibly the night we walked the Audubon trail. The upstairs neighbor and his kitten were driving you crazy, so you had built an elaborate soundproof shelter inside your bedroom, thick layers of insulation battened against your ceiling and walls, all of it covered with unpainted sheetrock, seams left untaped, nails exposed, a structure so cumbersome and crude you'd installed studs in the middle of the room to hold it all up. I was aghast. It was like a bunker, a fortress only a crazy person would build. I don't think anyone could have saved you.

What makes a difference for me is to know now that you were shooting morphine in the year before your death, more and more of it, and knew you were going to get caught. I won't say how I learned this, only that I find strange solace knowing that in the end you must have felt you had no choice. Or maybe it just allows me to let myself off the hook.

That was the difference between us. You could never grant yourself absolution. For you a single mistake always led to many. You forgave nothing. Your garden was perfect or else. Again I have tended mine past the new shoots and promise of spring. Again, despite all my efforts, wild morning glories have wound themselves through the tomatoes, black-eyed Susans, autumn sedum, and spent stalks of bee balm. Though I have pulled root after root, the pokeweed is heavy with berries, arching over the last daisies on its thick magenta stems. "Next year," I sigh like a Cubs fan, though I already know the smartweed, the spurge, smooth groundcherry, pigeon grass, and creeping Charlie will win. Even so, Tom, the gardens are lovely. Through the bay window I see you there still, hosing off storm windows, playing with our dogs, sitting on the park bench beside the pond where we said we'd have drinks one night but never did. That's my fault, of course, but I'm not like you were, I don't beat myself up. For me the past opens not like a wound but a flower, it all blooms again no matter the season, because the truth about memory is that one lie it *always* tells is time. We are young, we are healthy, there's gumbo on the stove as we gather at my table, our hands full of hope, we're studying the menu, buying the tickets, riding along Silas Creek Parkway in the sun, you are banking a shot, returning a serve, swinging the bat, cracking the spine of your latest Patrick O'Brian, smelling the ink and new paper in anticipation of the adventure inside, you are pulling a Lady Baltimore cake from the oven, nailing up a birdhouse, shaking out wet lettuce, tears run down your face as you laugh at Barney, Andy, and Aunt Bee, it's cocktail hour, it's spring, there are all the hours in the world, and you are in a time without time, a room without shadows, a handsome prince walking in a palace without walls.

And if that is too much, then let me be brief: We loved you.

Maybe that's all you wanted to hear. You must have wanted to hear something. Why else would you, so meticulous, so organized, always so particular about detail, have driven away from Cedar Street knowing you would never come back and left your answering machine on? Why else would you have said when I called on the morning of your service—don't ask me why—in that abrupt, inflectionless voice I had grown to dread, "You have reached 272-2783. Leave a message."

The Bride Beneath My Bed

THE BRIDE BENEATH my bed lives in a blue house with an awning, she lives in a cardboard coffin with a peephole, a big blue box with an eyelid, and looks out through the plastic window but never opens her eyes. She has no eyes, she has no face, I see this, there are no curtains, she just got married, she hasn't had time to hang them, I can lift the flap and spy on her whenever I want. I know it's her because her address is on the front, number 7, that was from the year she lived in storage, the year she moved out, but that's not true, she didn't move out, I'm the one who left her, left her beneath my bed and went off to sleep in a bed that had no bride, I went to grad school, I forgot her, and the groom got tired of her and kicked her out, sent her off to storage until the movers tracked me down and brought her back, she was like a homing pigeon, a real Lassie-come-home, that girl, no use trying to escape, she knew where she belonged, and she and her blue box crawled right back beneath my bed. It left its mark on her though, the year that she was gone, it's on her wall, that number 7, she was the seventh house on the storage block, the seventh box the groom evicted, he wrote the number out in Magic Marker, I recognize his writing. Maybe he was afraid that she'd get lost, he never did give her much credit, maybe she didn't deserve much, she got married too young, young and dumb, the way brides were supposed to be back then, so what do I expect? Before she was assigned a number she thought the curly dark blue and gold script was her address, *My Wedding Gown* it says, like those house numbers spelled out in fancy black wrought iron cursive, I had a friend once who liked to point them out, "They're trying to make you think that they can read," he said, but he wasn't fooled, not for a minute, neither was the groom, well he was fooled, must have been, for a minute anyway, but afterwards he forgot the way she used to read, she read Henry James and James Joyce, for fun she read Djuna Barnes, Virginia Woolf, William Faulkner, Vladimir Nabokov, and F. Scott Fitzgerald, she read Shakespeare, Sappho, Alexander Pope and e.e. cummings, she majored in English and minored in comp lit, but where's the paycheck in that, she needed a job, the groom was a graduate student, she would have a husband to support. So she got an office job, she hated it, but what else was she qualified to do, pasting labels on envelopes, anyone could do it, though it was so boring it wore her out, when she came home she cooked dinner, did the dishes, and put them all away, she did the laundry and mopped the floor, her reading must have slacked off, the groom thought so, he liked to laugh at her and say, "My wife's a big reader, every other week she looks up dogs in the encyclopedia." And well it's true she did like dogs, their apartment was no-pets, they got some fish, they named two gerbils and a turtle, the dog encyclopedia was a gift, he gave it to her, she was studying up for when he got his Ph.D. and she could get a puppy. So she had every reason to think *My Wedding Gown* was her number, her ID, it was where she lived, where she could be found, maybe she thought the letters meant that she was home and ready to receive callers, gentlemen callers, she read Tennessee Williams too, maybe that was her problem, she got married so young she hasn't made the transition from bride to wife, she's such an embarrassment, she thinks a bride is like a debutante all got up in a big white dress, she thinks the wedding is a coming-out party, like the high school prom no one asked her to, but that's not true, she did go with a boy she barely knew, his mother made him get a date, she wore a mint green dress, he gave her a green cymbidium orchid that looked so phallic she thought he must be making fun of her, but that's another story, all water over the dam and washed beneath the bridge now that she's a bride, look, her picture's in the paper, she's famous, barely old enough to vote and she's already had her fifteen minutes, and you know what happens then, it's all downhill from there, but don't tell her, she has no sense of time, she's like everyone else, she lost it inside her fifteen minutes, she hasn't noticed the clipping is crumbling, doesn't know the party's over, she won't take off her fancy white silk gown, though the guests have all gone home, they've moved away, they've gotten married and divorced, their children have married and divorced, they've gotten old, they've forgotten her, they've died, even the groom's gone on, it's been nearly fifty years, they were married less than ten when he booted her from beneath his bed and sent her off to storage, you'd think she'd get it, take the dress off, kick off her satin heels, put her feet up and take a load off, she could slip into something comfortable, an old flannel robe with a stain on the collar or a safety pin at the waist, no one's looking, the sheer white peignoir rotted years ago, the elastic in the sleeves went like an old rubber band, the nylon turned the color of jaundice, she can make herself a cup of tea and take her hair down, remove her makeup, scrub her face, she can relax now, no one's looking, and if they were? She's invisible, she's a ghost, who does she think would recognize her?

But maybe she's remembering the time when she wasn't sure she'd be a bride, that must be it, no one expected her to wed, but she fooled them, didn't she, all those neighbors who knew her when she was thirteen, so scrawny and awkward they could just look at her and see that she would never marry, she knew it, the boys all teased her so, it's lucky she didn't kill herself, lucky for her anyway, she was glad to go away to school, she had a scholarship, of course she did, she had no boyfriend to distract her, and when she left the woman on the corner told her mother that she was glad she wouldn't have to send her daughter to college because *her* daughter was so cute someone would marry her right away, and sure enough someone did, the bride beneath my bed was home on holiday, she went to the wedding, they played the polka, there was dancing in a big Polish hall, but no one asked her to dance, she came with her parents and didn't know anyone else there, except the bride of course, and her only slightly, the girl was two or three years younger, two or three years younger and already claimed—oh it looked grim for the bride beneath my bed, coming on her junior year of college with no prospects, and you know what happens when you graduate, her friends said, the odds go down, they plummet, if you don't have a ring by then you'll never have this chance to meet someone again.

But let's be fair, she's such an easy target, she had a boyfriend, she found one when she got to college, she could have married him, he talked about it all the time, it was all he talked about, their future, the four children they would have, they would marry as soon as they finished school, and then he planned to turn her into an automatic baby-making machine, he *said* this, she was the one who always changed the subject, the thought made her faintly ill, she thought it sounded like a Kenmore, she was seventeen years old, she wanted a boyfriend, she didn't want a husband and four children, she didn't even want to finish school to tell the truth, she liked school too much to want it to be over, she couldn't think that far ahead, she was a real seat-of-the-pantser, live-for-the-moment kind of girl, not that she was spontaneous, it was more that she was lazy, she procrastinated, she never thought to cross her bridges even when she came to them, she had no clue what she planned to do.

Her parents thought she should be a teacher, and why not if she liked school so much, but they must not have read the studies, the girls in the dorm read the studies, they knew. It was bad enough that the odds dropped so drastically upon receiving a diploma, teaching was the worst career a girl could choose, did she think the old maid schoolteacher was a joke, a myth, didn't she realize that the second she stepped up to the blackboard her chances would sink to less than one percent? She was more likely to be struck by lightning, she would be bitten by a shark, trampled by an elephant, sucked right out of the red-brick schoolhouse by a tornado, the Boston Strangler would escape from prison, Richard Speck would find her cowering beneath her bed, Charles Whitman would climb the Texas tower and fix her in his sights, she would board the Hindenburg, she would sail on the *Titanic*, a dam would burst and release the Johnstown Flood before she could find a husband. She might as well face facts: Ed McMahon will never come calling, Publishers Clearing House will lose her number, the van won't find her house, she will never be a winner, the odds are one in a gadzillion, if she wants to be a teacher she'd better find herself a new boyfriend quick.

Actually she didn't want to be a teacher, she took one education course, that was one too many, she refused to take another, she wasn't going to get her license after all, her parents were disappointed, but that was nothing new, she was a disappointing kind of girl, she was disappointed in herself, not about the teaching, it was everything else, though in her senior year she did begin to worry, graduation coming up and no job in sight, lucky for her a groom appeared at the last minute, spring of her senior year, already March, and there she was dallying with a man who would never settle down or marry anyone and what kind of investment was that? Her mother must have known as much, she was talking about having the bride beneath my bed come home to work at the telephone company, she could have her old bedroom back and pay room and board, the bride beneath my bed thought she'd rather die, but she should have thought of that sooner, shouldn't she, it's a lucky thing a groom came along when he did. She called her parents, her mother would be happy, she could invite the woman on the corner along with the daughter not yet twenty and already divorced, good thing she was so cute since she needed someone to marry her again, the bride beneath my bed felt lucky to get the chance just once, she was happy, why wouldn't she be, she would never have to worry about a date for Saturday night again. "I wish you'd known this boy a little longer," was what her mother said, and it was true, he was a boy, such a boy, she had no idea what a boy he was, a real live Peter Pan, but he was a cute boy, all her friends said so, the bride's mother could see for herself when they met at graduation.

So she didn't have to go home, she didn't have to leave the pretty college town that had once made her so happy, and it didn't matter what kind of job she got because she would be a student wife, that was her profession, she wouldn't have to use her brand-new degree, her liberal arts diploma, the useless and most prestigious kind for brides, luckily she could type, though the typing test was iffy, fifty words a minute, but they subtract the errors, so it was touch and go for her, though not hunt and peck, he was the hunt and pecker, she would have to type his papers, she could be a real support to him, his parents would see, they'd come around, look what a credit she would be with her English major, she would never embarrass him with bad grammar, she knew when to clap at the symphony and how to pronounce the names of all the painters at the museum, and anything else she needed to know he could teach her, because that's the way he was, a little snobbish, it wasn't his fault he grew up with money, it wasn't her fault she grew up without, his parents thought if her parents wouldn't buy her a fancy trousseau maybe the wedding should be put off, maybe he ought to marry a girl whose parents would, they too wished he had known her a little longer, actually they wished he had never known her at all, when he married her they gave him a car on the condition that she was never to drive it, why would he tell his father she wasn't a virgin?

The bride beneath my bed is still a virgin, she's untouched, sealed inside her blue box, she's slept beneath two husbands, but she's airtight, hermetic, vacuum packed, professionally preserved. Nothing penetrates, she's flawless, look at her pretty, virginal white dress. Luckily her mother didn't remember the dress she'd fallen in love with in a pattern book when she was ten, a dress dressed up like a birthday cake, a wedding cake, all ruffles and tiers, a real Cinderella gown, the kind of dress she could have dyed bright pink and worn to work at Cypress Gardens, but she was only ten, for heaven's sake, surely she can be forgiven her bad taste, she's got years to acquire some sophistication, years for her mother to forget where they put the pattern. So they went shopping, she tried on dress after dress, it was an important purchase, the bride beneath my bed will wear it her whole life, that boat-necked gown of sheer silk organza over a strapless taffeta shell, the bodice inlaid with Alençon lace, the skirt appliquéd with a sparkle of seed pearls and tiny crystals, a regiment of tiny silk-covered buttons marching down her back to disappear beneath her cathedral train and the flying buttress of its bow. She took the veil, that fountain of silk illusion capped by a headpiece of lace petals edged with pearls, in the center of her forehead a crystal teardrop like a Hindu bride's holy dot, a *bindi*, that circle of red powder. No one can say that she's not arrayed for the bridal, you could display her in a museum, she's a mummy now, wrapped up in her elaborate white winding cloth, her mother paid twenty-five dollars to preserve her inside her big blue house, her box, her archival wedding chest, just like King Tut in his tomb with a cobra over one eye and a vulture over the other, she's wrapped in her silk shroud and stuffed like a trophy fox, like a pheasant, a blue marlin, she'll last forever, only environmentally pure museum quality materials were used, her tissue-paper breasts are acid-free, so is the blue skin beneath the sheer silk shoulders, look at that, she's a blueblood after all. Personally I wonder if her breasts might be implants, she has health problems, she should sue, she can't breathe, she never eats, she has no appetite, her face is gone, she has no features, how is she supposed to wake up and smell the coffee or take a look around her? The crystal *bindi* hangs at the neckline of her dress, she can't hold her head up, she's like the women of Burma, the Padaung, who stack brass rings around their necks to attract rich husbands, to make their necks look longer, their muscles atrophy, they can't tip their heads to drink, if they take the rings off their heads collapse, they choke to death, it's a small price to pay for beauty. Maybe that's what happened, she died, suffocated inside her sealed blue box, her flesh has rotted, she decomposed, her neck and face have disappeared, she's like Miss Havisham, a relic, her wedding cake has calcified, the icing's full of cobwebs, there's nothing left of her but her dress. Still I wonder if she's wearing underwear, not the garter, the groom tossed that at the reception, but if you die do you still have to wear your strapless longline bra? She makes me think about my father-in-law, not the groom's father, the other one, the next one, when he died the undertaker asked did we want his pants on, only the top half of the casket was open, after all, but I was shocked, it seemed indecent, imagine burying your dad in a bare butt with coat and tie, we were so appalled we shined his cordovans and made the undertaker put his shoes on too.

 I don't know if the bride beneath my bed is wearing shoes, maybe she's barefoot, though she's not barefoot and pregnant I can tell you that, she's still a bride, not even a wife yet, she wants a puppy not a baby, though if she were pregnant I could undo her buttons, those hundreds of tiny silk-covered buttons, it's a good thing the train hid most of them, the day she got married they had to go undone. She should have known there'd be a crisis, it was a wedding after all, wedding planners advise the bride to carry safety pins for tears and baking soda to cover stains, and she was such a klutz we can expect that she would rip and spill, but let's give her this much, she didn't rip, she didn't spill, it was the hairdresser, the hairdresser who didn't show, it wasn't the bride's fault, she made the appointment, eight o'clock on a Saturday morning, she was getting married at eleven, and there she was in an empty salon with no one to do her hair but a janitor who showed her the appointment book with her name rubbed out. Lucky for her, her mother knew a woman with a shop in her basement, a stout middle-aged woman with a beauty operator's license and one chair, gave two Toni home permanents a year, hadn't learned a new style in twenty, but the bride beneath my bed was desperate, she had no choice, that was her problem, she never realized she had choices. So the woman did them one at a time, maid of honor first, washed and set and dried the waist-length hair, combed it out and said, "What am I supposed to do with *that*?" and piled a lumpy bun up on top of her head, it's a good thing the maid of honor was the bride's best friend, otherwise she would have left the bride beneath my bed waiting at the altar. Then the woman coifed the bride while the bride's mother took the maid-of-honor home to dress, she was sorry, the woman said, she wasn't used to working with long hair, it was the best that she could do, the bride's hair flipped out on one side and drooping on the other, good thing she had a veil, it was too late to do it over, so late they'd forgotten her, by the time she got home they'd all left for the church, she had to dress herself, it's a story to tell the grandkids, late to her own wedding. "Hurry up," her father said when they finally remembered her and sent him to get her, but she couldn't ask him to do up her buttons, could she, even if they'd had the time, lucky for her the train covered the ones she couldn't reach, what a story, hurry up, boys, sire some grandkids, she needs to pass the story on, she got married with her dress gaping beneath its silk swash of satin train.

You can bet those buttons are done up now though, she may have made her bed, but her mother paid twenty-five dollars for her to lie beneath it, paid a team of wedding gown specialists to clean her and preserve her, they're the ones who made her into the bride she is today. Her mother paid to remove the stains, but there were no stains, so they removed the stains you couldn't see, the latent stains, they pressed her and stuffed her and folded her inside her museum-quality house, its plastic window has no PVCs, the walls are acid-free, it was her mother's Christmas present to her along with a stack of dish towels and a frying pan, the kind of things they needed because the groom was still in school, when he finished the coursework for one Ph.D. he decided it wasn't what he wanted after all and started over on another, they didn't have a house, they would never have a house, they would move from apartment to apartment and never have an attic or a walk-in closet, the bride went to live beneath the bed because it was the only place they had to put her.

But it's not like she was in the way, who did she bother, it costs nothing to keep her, like free puppies to good homes, a bargain until you put up the fence and pay the vet bill, but it's worth it, she loves you, look at her wagging her tail and licking your face as she throws up on the sofa and chews the rug, the bride beneath my bed is much better behaved, she's a good girl, she's so good she's embarrassing, she's so good it's bad, she knows how to act, her mother taught her, though her mother would never approve of what goes on in the bed, it's not the sex, she's a married woman after all, it's the dog that sleeps there just like he's a person, her parents never let her have one growing up, she had allergies, not to mention dogs are dirty, when she washed the floor the groom came along behind her and said, "That's not the way my mother washes floors," he didn't think they could build a bookcase out of blocks and boards, it wasn't the way people did things, not people like his parents, but they had so many books in the end he came around, and when he sent her off to storage he kept the blocks and boards, he kept the books, he kept the antique ginger jars he bought her one summer in Hyannis, Cape Cod is where he always went for vacation as a child, so that's where they went, they had to sleep in her brother's old Cub Scout tent that didn't have a floor, it rained, they didn't have a lantern or a tarp, on clear nights they played miniature golf, they walked up and down the main street and watched the glass blower in the souvenir shop, he bought her the ginger jars, they drank liqueurs out of airplane bottles at the drive-in movie, during the day they rode bikes and swam, they never fought, it was like a honeymoon, did she think that meant it was like was a marriage?

So she didn't know what to expect, who does, what makes me think I would have been so much smarter? So what if she didn't know how to cook, she learned, didn't she, she wasn't the cook that I am now, but she wasn't bad, he even bragged about her pie crust to his mother, that was a mistake, his mother gave her used Crisco and told her to make a crust for apple pie, but the Crisco smelled like last night's fish, and when she said "I can't use this," his mother smiled, it made her so happy, "Of course you can," she said. So she let his mother trump her, she was too young to know how to throw her weight around, she didn't have much weight to throw, she was a lot thinner than I am, I'll give her that, her figure is much better, she's got more than a few things on me, her eyes are clear, her face is smooth, she has no cellulite or spider veins, she can turn a cartwheel, her feet don't hurt, her back is strong, her knees don't buckle, she has no trouble reading the fine print, her hair is still a lovely shade of auburn, it's not her fault one side hangs down and the other sticks out, she made the appointment, it was the hairdresser who played hooky, she should have washed her hair herself and pinned it in an updo, I look at her picture now and wonder why she didn't think of that, it would have looked good with her veil and crystal *bindi*, it's not too late, I could fix her in Photoshop, but why bother? No one's looking, and if they were who does she think would care? It's over, she's history, she's done with, sealed inside her box she has no hair, she never smiles, it's impossible to tell if she is happy, she has no face, she has no mouth, she has no voice, she never did, I think, and anyway what would she have had to say, she had no experience, she was just a girl, she never balanced her own bank account or filed her taxes, never raised a child, taught a class, or watched someone she loved die. She was never in charge of anything; she didn't even know how to drive. Who would hire her, she doesn't know how to use a computer, she's so out of it she still thinks that music comes on vinyl, it takes her an hour to bake a potato, she heats her leftovers in a 350-degree oven, she thinks you can mail a letter for five cents and fill a gas tank for three dollars, she banks in person, calls the operator to go long distance, and believes a restaurant is the only place you get a menu. She doesn't even know that she no longer lives beneath my bed, it's been years since I let her sleep there, I learned to drive, I went to grad school, I got a job, I bought a house, I married again, I had a son and gained a stepson, wrote some books and won some prizes, I kicked her out, I sent her upstairs, I got rid of her, she's not the bride beneath my bed anymore, she's the madwoman in my attic. What's happened to her is my fault, I didn't read the instructions, I didn't know she couldn't take the heat, it's an oven up there beneath the rafters, last time I saw her she was turning brown and brittle, she wasn't made to sleep in garrets, her blue archival home was meant to be a temporary shelter, I get that now, she wasn't supposed to be cast off, she was meant to be passed on, her mother must have hoped to watch her walk up the aisle again as a granddaughter one day, but the bride beneath my bed never had a daughter, she and Peter Pan got a puppy instead. I should have sold her, I could sell her still, for a price I could restore her, there are specialists who can bring a jaundiced bride's virginal whiteness back, but it costs too much, it's useless, there's no point, she's ruined, up there going mad, somewhere in that attic's worth of outgrown lives, the crib, the children's books, the report cards and roller blades, the tax returns, old clothes, golf clubs, and guitar, if I died what would my sons think, what would they make of her up there in her big blue box number 7? I need to find her, I can hold a yard sale, donate her to the Salvation Army, haul her to Goodwill. I'll do an autopsy I think, I'll open up her house, I'll let the air in, I'll find out what she's made of, find out what it was she lacked. She had a heart but was too young to read it, I can give her courage, I can offer her a brain, I'll tear away her cardboard walls, it's time that she got liberated, I'm done with her, I'll let her go. She's waiting, she's up there waiting patiently, though it frightens her to think that she might be discarded or sold, where would she go, she doesn't want to depend upon the kindness of strangers, she doesn't want to be set free, what she wants, all she wants—all she ever has—is for me to find her and say, *Hello. It's okay, you can stay with me, you're safe here. I remember you.*

Earlier versions of these essays first appeared in the following journals:

"The Village Idiot" in *The Gettysburg Review*
"Crossing the River" in *Shenandoah*
"Inside the Palace" as "I Cannot Write About You, I Can Only Write To You" in *The Southern Review*
"The Bride Beneath My Bed" in *Pleiades*

I am grateful to their editors and to Robert Atwan for naming each a Notable Essay of the Year in the annual Best American Essays anthologies.

My greatest thanks always to Michael Gaspeny, my partner in love, words, and memories for over fifty years, and to our sons, Al and Max. And finally my gratitude to Andrew Saulters and Unicorn Press for making this short book that means a great deal to me happen so beautifully.

LEE ZACHARIAS is the author of one previous collection of essays, *The Only Sounds We Make*, four novels, and a collection of short stories. She has received fellowships from the National Endowment for the Arts and the North Carolina Arts Council. Her work has received the Phillip H. McMath Book Award and the North Carolina Sir Walter Raleigh Award for Fiction, as well as recognition from the Independent Publisher Book Awards. Her first novel, *Lessons*, was a featured Book of the Month Club selection, and the Library of Michigan chose her third novel, *Across the Great Lake*, as a 2019 Notable Michigan Book.

Her novels have also been honored as distinguished favorites or finalists by the International Book Awards, New York City Big Book Awards, Pinnacle Book Achievement Awards, American Fiction Awards, USA Book Awards, National Indie Excellence Awards, the Omaha Book Prize, the Peter Taylor Prize for the Novel, and the Indies Foreword Awards.

Nearly all of her nonfiction (including the four essays collected here) has been cited in the annual Best American Essays, which reprinted her essay "Buzzards" in the 2008 collection. Co-editor of the anthologies *Intro 11* and *Runaway*, she has taught at the University of Arkansas, Princeton University, and the University of North Carolina Greensboro, where for ten years she served as director of the graduate writing program and editor of *The Greensboro Review*. She is married to poet and novelist Michael Gaspeny.

Text in Caslon. Titles in Arno.
Design by Andrew Saulters.

Unicorn Press produced 75
copies bound in boards and
425 bound in paper.